Business Culture in China

Yuan Wang

Xin Sheng Zhang

Rob Goodfellow

Published by Butterworth-Heinemann Asia, an imprint of Reed Academic
Publishing Asia,
a division of Reed Elsevier (Singapore) Pte Ltd
1 Temasek Avenue
#17–01 Millenia Tower
Singapore 039192

ISBN 9810089775

Cover design by Sam + Matt Design
Edited and typeset by Keyword Editorial Services
Printed by Kin Keong Printing Co. Pte. Ltd.

Foreword

It is with great pleasure that I commend this book as an important contribution to the development of a rapidly maturing relationship between China and the international business community. China is undergoing major and sometimes extraordinary changes in its economic and social structures, as are many of her major trading partners. This change has pushed forward unprecedented convergence in practically every field of human endeavour, including international trade and commerce.

The realities of constant change at the dawn of the 'era of globalisation' means that previously held stereotypical views about what constitutes a distinctive business culture must be constantly reexamined. Business culture in China is no different. The authors have presented a vivid picture of modern-day commerce in the People's Republic of China. Their evocative comments about 'information being like technology which can quickly become obsolete or irrelevant', and the importance of 'learning how to learn', as the essence of education in the era of globalisation, reflects a very practical approach to the study of modern-day China. *Business Culture in China* thankfully does not follow many other books that ill-advisedly attempt to 'explain' China's complex business culture in terms of tradition alone, but rather looks at business as a dynamic expression of a living, changing culture.

Business Culture in China creatively illustrates a number of key areas of interest that are seldom combined in one book. These areas include a discussion of Chinese managerial style, the best way to cooperate with various departments of the Chinese government, the skills of negotiation, the cultural 'essence' of Chinese commerce, Chinese consumer psychology and the most effective way of promoting goods and services in the 'world's largest market'.

I recommend the three authors, Dr Yuan Wang, Associate Professor Xin Sheng Zhang and Mr Rob Goodfellow, as extremely well qualified to write and comment on ways of increasing social understanding as well as trade between China and 'the outside world'. I enthusiastically support their efforts, and this important new book, as a timely contribution to the growing sense of mutual respect that is now bridging the 'cultural divide'.

Professor Michael Hough
Director MBA Program, The University of Wollongong

Contents

Preface

Since 1978 China has experienced nothing short of an economic miracle. In 20 years the Chinese people have created one of the strongest and most dynamic market economies in the world. The most important aspect of this new system is that it is not a carbon copy of other economic systems but rather has its own distinctively Chinese flavour. This emerging model will ensure future growth and prosperity for China well into the 21st century. With 1.2 billion people, the world's largest market, China will continue to provide enterprises of other countries with many exciting and profitable commercial opportunities.

How to successfully enter the Chinese market is the preoccupation of every foreign businessperson or manager presently interested in China. *Business Culture in China* addresses these questions in a timely and comprehensive fashion.

Dr Karen Yuan Wang is an expert in Chinese organisational management and business culture. She has a great deal of both theoretical and practical experiences in comparative Western and Chinese business cultures, particularly in respect to marketing and management.

Associate Professor Xin Sheng Zhang is one of China's foremost researchers and practitioners of Public Relations Theory, and the pioneer of the Chinese Corporations Identity System. He has published many works in these fields. Professor Zhang's publications have had a profound influence in the field of management in China. Further, Professor Zhang's work has generated a great deal of further research into related fields.

Rob Goodfellow is a Western researcher who understands the business cultures of South-east and North-east Asia. His experience and knowledge of the region is rich and insightful. He is well published in his field, having produced an important work entitled *Indonesian Business Culture* (Butterworth-Heinemann, Singapore,1997).

Significantly, all three authors have been exposed to both Western and Eastern cultures: in this sense they are culturally bilingual. As a crystallisation of the authors' experiences and research, this book constitutes an important contribution to cross-cultural understanding. It provides readers with deep insights into Chinese business culture from a uniquely inside angle. It will be a valuable tool for those Western businesspeople or managers who wish to enter and then succeed in the Chinese market. I congratulate the publisher, Reed Academic Publishing, for their commitment to promoting regional goodwill and cultural knowledge. I am certain that the authors' efforts will be well appreciated by the many hundreds of thousands of business people presently fascinated by the Chinese market.

Finally, on behalf of the Chinese Marketing Association (CMA), I would like to offer prospective foreign clients, partners, associates and friends the opportunity to access the wide range of high quality CMA consultant services and training programmes. Members of the CMA, as China's peak marketing body, sincerely believe that these programs will build on the process of cultural and commercial understanding initiated by Wang, Zhang and Goodfellow in *Business Culture in China*.

Jia Lu-Rang
Professor, Institute of Finance, Trade & Economics/ Graduate School , The China Academy of Social Sciences
Standing Vice President, Chinese Marketing Association
Senior Commercial Consultant for the Government of the People's Republic of China

Professor Jia Lu-Rang is a well-known marketing expert and senior consultant for a number of large state-owned and public companies in China. He has published a range of books on many aspects of the emerging market in China and on marketing strategies. Professor Jia Lu-Rang is the author and coordinator of a major research initiative entitled 'The Socialist Market Model', a project sponsored by the Chinese government. The recommendations arising from this research have become an important reference point for policy makers and planners in the China. Professor Jia Lu-Rang Jia passed away unexpectedly in January 1998. This book is dedicated to his memory.

About the Authors

Yuan Wang is a lecturer, project manager and consultant who specialises in Chinese business culture and international management. Dr Wang (Ph.D., Management) has extensive knowledge of China's organisational culture and market, based on a 10-year career in business operations. She has consulted to private corporations and governmental organisations in both China and Australia. Dr Wang has conducted extensive research into comparative modes of management, negotiations and human resources of joint ventures in China and internationally. As an expert consultant in these fields, Dr Wang enjoys a close relationship with business, professional associations and the media in China.

Dr Wang has also taught at postgraduate level (MBA) in both the People's University of China (PUC), the People's Republic of China, and the University of Technology Sydney, Australia. She held the position of Deputy Director (1990–92) in the Institute of Foreign Economy and Management, the PUC. She has produced a number of articles and books in the fields of management and business culture.

Xin Sheng Zhang is an Associate Professor in the Faculty of Adult Education, at the People's University of China, the People's Republic of China, Beijing. Professor Zhang has conducted extensive research on macro-economics in the People's Republic of China on behalf of the Research Institute (Economic and Management System Reform), of the State Commission for Restructuring the Economic System, and the China Corporate Culture Association.

Professor Zhang was one of the first scholars in the People's Republic of China to research and apply the theory of Public Relations to both the Chinese academic and corporate fields. He has since delivered a number of keynote academic addresses on the subject, broadcast through China Central

Television Station (CCTV) and the China National Radio Network (CNR).

Professor Zhang has published many books and articles in the field of Chinese corporate culture and public relations in the People's Republic of China. He has been involved in marketing consultancy for many large companies in both China and overseas since 1987. Currently, Professor Zhang is the Deputy Chairman of the Australian–Chinese Science and Technology Association and a Senior Consultant with both Austar Public Relations Pty Ltd and SES Pacific Investment Group Pty Ltd.

Rob Goodfellow is an Australian-based author, researcher and consultant who has extensive experience in the field of Indonesian and Chinese business cultures. Through Rob's continued association with the University of Wollongong, Monash Mt. Eliza Business School and the Indonesian Islamic University in Yogyakarta, Rob continues to be involved in the gathering, cross-referencing and analysis of sensitive commercial, social and political data. He is the author of many journal, magazine and newspaper articles and the author of *Indonesian Business Culture* (Butterworth-Heinemann, Singapore, 1997).

In 1995–97 Rob acted as senior consultant to a number of Chinese business conglomerates. In this capacity he developed a high degree of organisational and problem-solving skills in the area of joint venture cooperation.

Rob is presently working with Dr Muhammad Akhyar Adnan at the International School at the Department of Economics, the Islamic University of Indonesia, on a project that will compile an international database of Islamic banking and financial products. Ultimately this project will culminate in the publication of two books related to the subject. The project is scheduled to complete in March 1999.

Rob is currently researching a PhD project, which looks at history and memory in contemporary Indonesia. The project is entitled *'Sing Wis, Ya Wis*—What is Past is Past'. It involves the development of new analytical tools by which to understand the nature of contemporary memory in the historical process.

Acknowledgements

Special thanks to Mr Fan-sheng Gou, Chairman of the Huiecong Group, and Ms Qing Zhang, Senior Executive, Huiecong Group for professional assistance with current Chinese market data; Professor Michael J. Hough; Miss Ji-nong Wang; Mr Jin-Ju Yin; Ms You-de Shi, Mrs Helen Naylor; Mr You-wen Song.

A final expression of thanks to Ms Ying Gou for contributing her drawings for chapter titles.

This book is dedicated to the memory of Professor Jia Lu-Rang.

Introduction

The Dragon Awakes

The Chinese believe that the Great Dragon ruled the Middle Kingdom of the world for nearly four thousand years. For most of this period China was a great trading nation. Then the dragon fell asleep for two centuries, while China collapsed under the coopting and erosive effects of colonialism, until in 1978 the late Paramount Leader Deng Xiao Ping, in a sense, woke the dragon up. And as the world now knows, the Chinese Dragon is back, hungry to take her place as the economic and cultural superpower of the 21st century.

The Cultural Divide

Notwithstanding all the optimism about what is often called the world's largest market, anyone who is actually operating a company in China will tell you that there are still many problems with China's present economic and bureaucratic systems. Indeed, the road to cross-cultural cooperation has been a difficult one. Often the significant differences that exist between what we broadly identify as either 'Chinese' or 'Western' values have not been thoroughly examined or anticipated by foreign businesspeople before commercial engagement. This cultural divide is most pronounced in terms of discrete social, political and economic models, but also involves issues of tradition, world-view and belief systems. Some differences are surprisingly contemporary in origin. For instance, from 1949 until 1978 China was essentially isolated from the forces of capitalist trade liberalisation and global economic reform. The result of this was that while the rest of the world was experiencing profound change, the Chinese economic dragon was only just starting to wake from its long sleep. In this way, misunderstandings between China and the West also involve perceptions of business practice in the context of late capitalism and globalisation.

For these and other reasons, many of China's prospective trading partners still feel genuine apprehension about committing themselves to the Chinese market. This poses something of a dilemma. In recent years most Western-based, export-oriented companies have come to the conclusion that China cannot be ignored. But on the other hand many find Chinese business culture so confusing that they resist establishing formal trade links. Consequently, when decisions are made to test the market, fundamental differences of opinion, or rather perception, tend to characterise almost all preliminary trade or investment discussions. How this situation is managed determines whether planning proceeds or becomes hopelessly lost in a maze of mutual confusion or conflict. Experience has shown that without proper preparation this unfortunate scenario is inevitable.

Clearly China remains a great mystery to most foreign businesspeople (as the West is for most Chinese). In many respects these two societies are really discrete worlds, or parallel civilisations, which before the colonial period developed in almost complete isolation from each other. And when these worlds did meet it was through the one-sided experience of European colonisation. It is not surprising then that mutual misunderstanding between actual or potential business partners and investors often occurs, despite the continued integration of the world economy.

The fundamental issue of basic social acclimatisation is a prerequisite that must be mastered before you can begin to feel confident with more complex issues. Understanding Chinese business values and the characteristics of Chinese business culture is a challenging though not impossible project. Many Western people succeed brilliantly in their efforts to do so. However, for most businesspeople there remain a number of fundamental barriers to overcome. Language is a good example. Basic concepts, particularly in business, are often improperly translated across cultures. Sometimes understanding and agreement are wrongly presumed because the English-language fluency of a Chinese negotiator is overestimated, or it is incorrectly accepted that a Chinese counterpart understands Western culture. These are all risky presumptions.

Unifying Factors

Another important theme that underpins *Business Culture in China,* and which helps to explain some of the changes in contemporary Chinese society, is national pride. The Chinese are a proud and ancient people who have suffered the indignity of almost two centuries of colonialism, first European and then Japanese. Because of this, in their hearts they do not approve of non-Chinese telling them what to do. This is especially true of confronting, unbalanced or unilateral criticism, particularly of domestic, economic or political policy. This sentiment is seldom expressed, but always deeply felt. It can be seen in business, but of course in the politics of international relations as well. To counter this, *Business Culture in China* has been written from an insider's perspective.

The predominance of this sense of national pride in China today is easy to explain. The Chinese are only now redefining their national dignity after the humiliation of foreign conquest and colonisation. The Chinese people will not so easily forfeit their self-respect again. In fact most Chinese will exert their newfound pride and confidence at every opportunity. This is seen in the wave of national pride that has practically eclipsed state ideology as the engine of Chinese society.

National pride has in fact been the driving force behind economic and cultural revitalisation since 1978. It was also the predominant official discourse in the years and months leading up to China's historic reunification with Hong Kong in 1997. Significantly, the reason for China's marked emphasis on the integrity of the Chinese nation-state is that most Chinese see their country as a type of human body: in this way Hong Kong was, as Macao and Taiwan still are, amputated parts which must be returned to ensure the wholeness of nation. The wave of pride that swept China following the return of Hong Kong is evidence that the restitution of China's dignity is still an important issue. Hong Kong is also evidence that the Chinese have long memories.

In Beijing this sense of history and restitution was, and continues to be, promoted at every level of government and society. *The Peoples' Daily* in Beijing, for example, called the Hong Kong hand-over 'a centennial event for the Chinese nation'. The pride associated with the hand-over was typified by the words of one leading Chinese academic who commented that the 'event expunged centuries of humiliation'. National pride then is expected to continue to be a prominent discourse in China well into the 21st century as the administration of President Jiang Zemin looks for new ways of accommodating China's search for nation-state integrity.

However, traditional, historical, cultural and current views of the Chinese state, while foundational and essential, are merely the means to an end, not a destination in itself. Current cultural information should be seen as the raw material of genuine understanding. Anyone who wants to enter the Chinese market, or just wants to know more about China's dynamic present, can learn to craft their own approach by carefully considering the content of *Business Culture in China*, and applying these lessons to fresh challenges in an ever-changing, fluid situation.

Learning to Learn about China

China is now in the middle of a revolution. Indeed, change has been so dramatic that everyone finds it difficult to adapt to alterations in government policy. In this, you must be wary of accepting information about China as cultural preparation. Information is not necessarily understanding. Information, like technology, can quickly become obsolete or irrelevant. The important point is that base-line knowledge about traditional and current business culture in China is a tool with which to develop specialsied expertise in one particular aspect of the Chinese market.

In this context, a book about Chinese business culture must be careful not to fall into the trap of claiming to be able to 'explain' China. China is far too complex to be comprehensively 'understood'. We have produced a uniquely Chinese perspective on life and commerce in China with the aim of equipping non-Chinese businesspeople to design their own personal and professional analytical tools, which can be applied to new tasks as they arise. This will assist you in developing your own China-related field of commerce. Corporate objectives can then be determined and the process of designing specific strategies can begin.

China is a rich and complex social mosaic. Often it is only one small part of the mosaic that is relevant, or indeed comprehensible. For instance, the experience of a footwear manufacturer will be very different from that of insurance or investment broker, a fresh food exporter or a company that transfers infrastructure technology. While all will be aiming at market penetration, everyone must enter China by a different door, each of which has its own particular key. This then is the challenge of 'learning how to learn', which is the essence of education, particularly in the era of globalisation. *Business Culture in China* meets this challenge.

To fulfil the demand for information about China, many excellent texts have been written by China specialists. These attempt to explain, in great detail, how to be successful in the Chinese market. Many have focused on explaining the fundamentals of

Chinese civilisation. However, in some cases, they merely answer big-picture questions, which are not relevant to the real world of business. Because of this, some of the most important aspects of business culture are overlooked in the search for meaning, or worst still, the practical current cultural context is lost in an all-encompassing theory of China. The key, however, is to integrate the theoretical and practical into one comprehensive, succinct, and easy-to-read guide. *Business Culture in China* is written from this perspective, concentrating on how best to operate in the Chinese market in spite of change. This business-like approach, based on certain core values (which partially transcend the inevitable turmoil of modernisation), is the way Chinese themselves cope with modern life.

Business Culture in China

The 'Chinese way' is the subject of subsequent chapters. It will provide a practical and comprehensive understanding of both the strategies and the skills required for doing business and keeping ahead of change in China. We answer a number of key questions. These include what features characterise traditional Chinese business culture? How has this changed? In what way does Chinese managerial style differ from the West? How do you best cooperate with various Chinese governmental departments? What is the most effective way of negotiating? What is the essence of the Chinese market? How do you explain Chinese consumer psychology? How do you use the Chinese custom of gift-giving to increase your interpersonal and professional effectiveness? What role do banquets play in Chinese business activities? How should you effectively promote your products and services in China? The answers to these questions are particularly relevant to export-orientated companies that want to find their way in the Chinese market. Indeed, China's remarkable level of economic activity and robust demand for a vast range of goods and services makes these questions and the Chinese market difficult to ignore.

What now makes China even more difficult for foreign investors to overlook is the fact that China has so far weathered the 1997–98 Asian financial crisis. One of the reasons that China has not suffered as badly as other Asian countries is that its economic fundamentals and reform policy are considered to be 'basically on the right track by the International Monetary Fund (IMF) and the World Bank.

But before we examine these issues, we should remind ourselves that while China's future is full of promise and prospects, the present is at times disorienting. You need to step back and examine the cultural and historical basis for China's unique civilisation, to identify some of the general but fundamentally consistent features of business culture in China. Graduated preparation will give you the confidence to navigate the unfamiliar terrain of a new and ever-changing business dynamic. It will give you the ability to carve out you own particular field of China expertise. From this point you can go on and make useful knowledge-building generalisations about Chinese business—from a uniquely 'inside' cultural perspective.

Chapter One

Chinese Trade and Business

History and Development

Since 1978 China has consistently pursued what has been termed an 'Open Door' policy to international trade and investment. Implementation of the late Deng Xiao Ping's discrete programme of economic reform has clearly brought about remarkable changes in China's economy, politics and culture. The pace of success of these reforms has greatly impressed China's trading partners, and has amazed the Chinese people themselves. However, it is necessary to realise that modern China's experience with international trade did not start with the reforms of 1978.

The 'Glory' and the 'Backwardness' of China's Trade History

China is an ancient civilisation, with a homogeneity of culture that spans the centuries from about 2500 BC to the present day.

The Silk Road

As early as the second century BC, Chinese Han Dynasty traders established commercial links across half the globe. From this time until the early 19th century, China was indisputably a great trading nation.

The first and most dynamic period of Chinese commercial expansion occurred during the Tang Dynasty (618–907 AD). At this time merchants traded goods internationally along a route that has become known as the Silk Road. The Silk Road began in Xi-An, the Capital of China during the Tang Dynasty (and still the capital of the present-day Province of Shan Xi). The route then snaked westward, exiting China near Ka-shi, in the present-day Province of Xin-Jiang, and continued on through to Russia, Northern India, Afghanistan and Persia, finally ending in the port city of Tyre, in what is now Lebanon. From Tyre goods were traded across the length and breath of Europe. During this prosperous era, Chinese, Middle Eastern and European merchants, adventurers, missionaries and officials all travelled the Silk Road, trading with each other in goods such as silken cloth, spices, tea and chinaware.

China's next period of rapid expansion occurred during the Ming Dynasty (1368–1644 AD). Between 1405 and 1433, Chinese merchants conducted seven commercial voyages to the ports of South-east Asia and West Africa with the specific purpose of expanding Imperial China's trading power and influence. The first of these expeditionary voyages involved 62 ships and 27 870 men, including representatives of the Imperial Court, clerks, accountants and buyers. These journeys brought great wealth and prestige to China and clearly demonstrated China's capacity to trade internationally.

In the early 16th century, European trading vessels began to arrive in mainland China. In 1557 Portuguese merchants were given permission to establish a commercial base in Macao. Thereafter, something of a trade war ensued, with British and Dutch companies seizing every opportunity to challenge Portuguese influence. It was during this period, the late Ming and early Qing Dynasties, that China first attempted to limit the influence of the outside world.

The Price of Closing China's Door to the World

This 'closed door' mentality first appeared in China at a time when the West was rapidly industrialising. While Europe's global influence was spreading, China became preoccupied or perhaps enchanted with its past glories. Weakened by internal turmoil, discontent, and corruption, the Imperial Qing government became self-satisfied with China's archaic economy. The affluent and exclusive Imperial Court had little interest in accepting anything from the West, let alone industrial technology.

In 1793, King George III of Britain sent a senior emissary on a deputation to the Court of Emperor Qianlong in Beijing to request the use of an off-shore island depot as a potential trading base with China. The deputation was treated coldly. The Qing government largely refused to open its door to foreign trade, with the exception of small-scale operations in Guangdong Province.

Despite this setback, 18th- and 19th-century British commerce with China increased 15-fold in China's favour, mostly in the trade of silk and tea. This negative balance of trade was a constant problem for the British. In the early 19th century Britain seized on an imaginative solution: they began exporting opium to China. The tragedy of the opium trade was immediately obvious. As the drug poured into China, and as the number of opium addicts rapidly increased, British opium merchants and others became wealthy and influential. Meanwhile China was distracted morally, socially and economically. The Qing government's response to this disaster was to abruptly end most trading activities with the West, thus effectively closing China's door to the outside world. The Imperial Qing Court arrogantly rejected all outside influence, vigorously pursuing a policy of commercial and cultural isolation.

In 1840 this isolation was challenged by military means. The humiliation visited on the Chinese people during the so-called Opium War demonstrated the West's clear military and technological superiority. The shame of this period was made even more acute by the fact that China was carved up by some 19 foreign countries as they joined the scramble for spheres of influence, concessions and protectorates in the 10 years before the final collapse of the Qing Dynasty in 1911. These nations included Britain, France, the United States, Russia and Japan, but also lesser players such as Peru, Brazil and Mexico, who all concluded hostilities with unequal 'treaties' that guaranteed open access to markets. It was probably only because of the jealousy and mutual antipathy of competing foreign imperialists that China was spared the type of partition that saw the African continent divided into colonial vassal states.

The Imperial Qing Court realised that it must appropriate Western expertise if it was to maintain any vestige of economic power, military advantage or sovereignty. Chinese merchants from Fujian Province first responded by importing processing equipment from the West in 1861 in an attempt to add value to their chief export commodity—tea. From 1861, official Chinese government merchants began purchasing advanced equipment in order to lay the foundations for a modern industrial society. This included railway, shipping, communications and manufacturing expertise and equipment.

Actually the Qing government was more interested in importing vast quantities of Western military technology in order to prepare a defence against the West. Ironically this was part of what became known as the 'Self-Strengthening Movement', a positive response to the isolationist policies of the Qing Dynasty and an attempt to re-open the door to international trade. It was also an attempt to protect China's sovereignty.

Gunboat diplomacy

However, during this open door period, trade between China and the West was not underwritten by mutually beneficial commerce, but by military force—or, as it become known, 'Gunboat Diplomacy'. The military pre-eminence of Europe ensured that China was forced into signing a variety of unequal treaties. China was subsequently divided up into spheres of influence—British, European, American, Japanese and so on. These humiliating relationships were compounded by the Japanese military victory in the Sino–Japanese War of 1894, which ended with China's crushing defeat.

The corrupt and incompetent late Qing Dynasty argued that the Self-Strengthening Movement had been a failure, and that the introduction of Western technology had not saved China from its decline or defeat at the hands of the Japanese military. Hence, senior state functionaries argued that traditional Chinese culture was the only effective weapon for resisting the invasion of foreign powers, ideas, culture and trade. Traditionalists turned back to ancient practices, political conservatism and a fanatical hatred of the 'foreign devils'. Outside influence was again severely restricted.

New isolationism: the door remains closed

The history of China from the late colonial period until the Chinese Revolution in 1949 was one of invasion, conquest and civil war. However, after 1949 a programme of internal reconstruction and industrialisation did actually revitalise the Chinese economy, with an average growth rate of 750% between 1949 and 1978. Unfortunately, this was the Cold War era, and China essentially remained quarantined from the fundamental economic reorganisation that was sweeping the rest of the world. This was particularly true of the 10 years between 1966 and 1976, the Cultural Revolution, when China was completely isolated from non-communist developed nations.

During the Cultural Revolution, domestic commercial activities were tightly controlled by the government, with private business regarded as one of the 'devils' of capitalism. As a result, China fell well behind the rest of the world in industry, technology and managerial skills, and its overall standard of living fell. For example, in 1965 Shanghai's gross domestic product (GDP) was higher than that of Hong Kong, but by 1976 Hong Kong's economy towered over that of Shanghai. Clearly the Closed Door Policy as it emerged during the Qing Dynasty, and as it peaked during the Cultural Revolution, visited backwardness and disaster on China's society and economy.

The Miracle of China's Economic Development in the Late 20th Century

The Open Door Policy

China's door to international trade swung open again in 1978. Significantly on this occasion the Open Door was a deliberate policy initiative of a sovereign government, not the result of Gunboat diplomacy. The Open Door, as initiated by the late Paramount Leader Deng Xiao Ping, was a conscious action, supported by the majority of the Chinese people. Its great achievement was that it comprehensively addressed the wrong policy of previous governments, even dating back to the Qing Dynasty. The Chinese people clearly recognised that industrial modernisation, the adoption of advanced methods of agriculture and the opening up of international trade was the only way China could assume its place as a modern, prosperous nation.

'Mind Liberalisation'

Part of this process involved what is now known as 'mind liberalisation'—a type of social and theoretical change that became the necessary prerequisite for the rapid development of China's modern market economy. 'Mind liberalisation', as part of the 1978 Open Door reforms, led many policy makers to openly challenge contemporary Stalinist economic doctrines, particularly towards the end of the Cultural Revolution. It challenged the pre-eminence of a centralised planned economy, the control of business enterprise by government, the general suppression of commercial activities and the law of absolute averages which discriminated against the concept of profit in commerce. This shift in attitudes has changed the way most Chinese think about business. The majority now acknowledge that commerce can and does make a very positive contribution to the nation. A healthy economy, a better standard and quality of living for all Chinese and the security of a confident sovereign state are the result of 'Mind Liberalisation' and an Open Door policy to foreign trade and investment. This consensus of opinion established a stable base on which to construct reform in China. From these foundations China has been able to dramatically absorb new technology and expertise and ultimately compete in the global marketplace.

China's Economic Miracle

The reform policies of the late Deng Xiao Ping have served the goal of economic growth well. China has experienced something of an economic miracle, with an annual average growth rate in GDP of 9% over 18 years since 1979—see Figure 1.1.

Economic reform has seen China's exports grow from US$18.27 billion in 1980 to US$ 151.1 billion in 1996, an increase of 8.27 times. China's total imports and exports are at present (1997) running at US$325 billion, constituting ninth

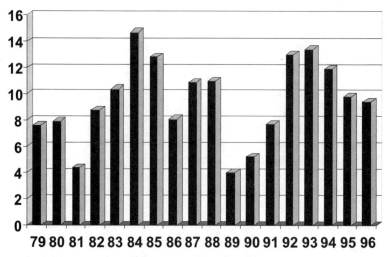

Figure 1.1 China's GDP from 1979 to 1996
(Source: China State Statistical Bureaux)

place overall in the ranking of the world's most successful trading nations. With the return of Hong Kong to China in July 1997, China is now the fourth largest trading country in the world behind the USA, Japan and Germany, with an overall trade surplus of US$40.3 billion (in 1997).

In 1996, with a GDP growth rate at 9.7%, China's domestic investment in fixed assets was measured at US$284.68 billion, an increase of 18.2% from 1995. During this period China's national savings also reached US$464.41 billion, an increase from US$96.5 billion in 1995. Clearly this high level of domestic savings provides China with a huge capital base.

China Encourages Foreign Investment

Attracting foreign capital has been an important aspect of China's reform policy since the Chinese Department for Industry and Commerce began accepting the registration of foreign companies and liaison offices in 1980. Consequently, China is now the world's fastest growing economy and one of the world's most attractive markets for capital investment. Major investors are drawn from Japan, Hong Kong (now a special administrative region), the United States, Germany, France and Taiwan. In the period between 1980 and 1997, China attracted a total of US$212.12 billion in capital investment from a staggering 300 000 foreign joint venture companies. (Significantly the average foreign investment per project was worth US$3.36 million.) Moreover, contracted investment is currently running at US$510 billion. According to a report from the Trade and Development Section of the United Nations, China's capital inflow is now ranked second place in the world, behind the United States. As a result, in 1997 the Chinese Government achieved an 8.8% growth rate of GDP and US$305.1 billion in domestic investment of fixed assets, with China's foreign exchange reserve reaching US$140 billion, ranking second in the world after Japan.

Towards Economic Superpower Status: China in the 21st Century

In 20 years China has undergone a complete transformation from a sleeping, introverted giant into a dynamic global force. This has lead the Organisation for Economically Developed Countries (OECD) to predict that by 2015 China will surpass the United States as the world's largest purchaser of goods and services.

As evidence to support this optimistic projection, the industriousness of the Chinese people is certainly a key critical factor. So is China's relatively high level of general education, as well as the country's enviable national savings programme, which at 35%–40% of gross domestic product is over twice the average rate of most Western nations. Nevertheless, the main reason why international business is fascinated with the Chinese market is that China possesses over 15% of the world's population. China's population is in fact more than the sum of the populations of the European Community and the North American Free Trade Zone. There are 335 million people in the European Community and 360 million in the North American Free Trade Zone—China's population is currently 1.2 billion. This makes China the world's largest market.

Clearly this market is taken seriously by the West. China's impressive 20-year average 9% rate of economic growth has been fuelled by a massive inflow of foreign capital and expertise. In the period between 1980 and 1994, more than 45 000 foreign companies established subsidiaries in China, to the extent that most of the world's corporate flagships are now represented. In addition, many Western-based overseas Chinese-owned companies are now operating successfully in China. Well-connected entrepreneurs, who were practically excluded from commercial activity in China before 1978, have established close ties with their ancestral homeland. This international network of Chinese capital has further diversified and strengthened the nation's economy.

With the further development of the Chinese economy, steady improvements in political relations between China \ _ the West, the Chinese market is expected to open up even further. And as it does, foreign companies and their Chinese joint-venture partners will enthusiastically seek to identify and exploit any realistic or achievable commercial opportunity. Indeed, more and more Western companies and businesspeople have recognised this, and are eager to enter the Chinese market.

Based on rapid economic growth, the rate of China's urbanisation is also accelerating. According to a statistical report of the Ministry of Construction, the number of cities has increased 650 times since 1980. The urban population has reached 350 million, with the rate of urbanisation currently standing at 30%. There are now 75 large, 192 medium and 399 small cities in China. Forty per cent of these cities are located in eastern China, 37% are in central China, and 19% in western China. According to an official estimate, by the year 2000 there will be over 800 cities in China. With an urbanisation rate of over 60%, the urban population will increase to 800 million. China's huge market and the trend towards continuous urbanisation will make it even more attractive for trade and investment.

Furthermore, a recent International Monetary Fund (IMF) study found that much of China's economic growth since 1978 has been due to increases in total productivity. This is not only because of improvements in technology, but also because of an increase in capital expenditure and labour output. To an extent this was reflected in China's agricultural employment rate, which dropped from 70% in 1978 to 54% in 1994, while employment in industry and the service sector increased. This has lead to a reallocation of labour into higher value-added activities. Even in township and village enterprises, privately owned operations are encouraged to focus on the bottom line. Investment in joint ventures and foreign enterprises has further led to an improvement in management effectiveness and increased productivity. Clearly China's exposure to international competition has indirectly increased the productivity and growth of its enterprises through export. It has been estimated that this rate of economic growth will continue well into the 21st century.

A basis for this optimism is clearly illustrated by examining the Communist Party of China's 15th Congress held in Beijing during September 1997. The Congress was actually a watershed for continued economic and political reform—but, as outlined, reform according to a uniquely Chinese perspective. President Jiang Zemin made it very clear that a strong and confident state system was the best means of achieving what China needs most—a structured rule of law and an efficient and transparent bureaucracy.

President Jiang Zemin outlined that in the next two years enterprise management reform will involve the planned restructuring of some 300 000 state-owned enterprises. These will ultimately present foreign investors with new opportunities to invest in the 103 000 state-owned enterprises in the industrial sector alone as particular enterprises are incorporated into the capitalist sector. These reforms will signal an exciting new era of trade opportunities, particularly in the services sector—all, however, implemented according to 'the Chinese way'.

This chapter has considered the role of commerce in Chinese history, and compared this to the change that occurred in the Chinese economy after 1978. The next chapter will put this change into the context of Confucianism and old business values, many of which are considered both relevant and consistent with reform in China today.

Chapter Two

Chinese Business Values of the Past

Confucian Influence

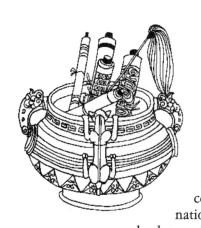

Confucius was born around 2500 BC in the small State of Lu, located in modern-day Shandong Province. The cornerstone of Confucianism concerns the governance of a nation—China incidentally was in absolute political and social turmoil during Confucius' lifetime. Based on his ideas, the belief system we know as 'Confucianism' developed to become the dominant cultural influence in China for over 2000 years.

Confucianism

Confucianism maintains that the entire complex of 'moral convention' is the cement of society. Convention can be differentiated into five major areas of importance:

- hierarchy
- collectivism
- 'face' protection
- respect for tradition or age
- egalitarianism.

These values must be appreciated as central to any study of Chinese national values and their particular influence on ways of doing business today.

Hierarchy

Western and Chinese cultural values have different origins. For many reasons—historical, cultural and religious—Western culture has nurtured the concept of relative social equality, such as equality 'in the sight of God' or equality of opportunity for individual effort in every field of human endeavour, including trade. Over time this has created the cultural and psychological basis for democratic consciousness.

In contrast, Chinese cultural values originate from a civilisation that developed in a continental environment and prospered by agriculture rather than maritime trade. Chinese civilisation subsequently developed around the common interests of the family as the pre-eminent economic unit, not the city-state as in Europe. Chinese culture is actually built on 'the family state', a form of social organisation that is autocratic and hierarchical, and not at all democratic.

Confucianism came into existence in order to provide a particular ruler with a basic theory of how to govern a troubled nation. Confucianism maintains that only a distinct hierarchy, in which each lower level gives obedience to a higher level, can guarantee the steadiness of a country and ultimately safeguard the power of a particular ruler. Confucianism uses family hierarchy to support societal hierarchy. Confucius used the term *li* to represent a comprehensive range of social obligations, imposed by the highest order of courtesy and moral duty, which was tested against a range of discrete relationships. He subsequently identified five basic human relationship categories, which he called *wu lun*: Emperor (kindness) – Subject (loyalty); Father (protection, consideration) – Son (respect and obedience); Husband (obligation) – Wife (submission); Older Brother (care) – Younger Brother (modelling subject) and finally; Friends or Friendship (trust).

Relationship	Representing	With	Representing
Emperor	kindness	Subject	loyalty
Father	(protection, consideration)	Son	respect and obedience
Husband	obligation	Wife	submission
Older brother	care	Younger brother	modelling subject
Friend	trust	Friend	trust

A traditional Chinese principle maintains that 'if an Emperor asks a subject to forfeit his life, then the subject must do so without question; and a son must sacrifice himself, if his father asks him to do so'.

Nowadays in China a profound hierarchical pattern is still mirrored in society. For example, superiors and subordinates in the workplace, as well as senior officials and ordinary people, all consider each other essentially unequal. The entire Chinese social system is based on existential inequality. Subordinates, or 'ordinary people', expect to be told what to do. Politics in China and the machinations of the Chinese bureaucracy and state-owned enterprises are practically incomprehensible without first understanding this key point.

Confucianism further justifies the ethical significance of a hierarchical system by claiming that society is governed by a number of key moral norms. These include:

- loyalty (*zhong*)
- piety (*xiao*)
- kindness (*ren*)
- obligation (*yi*)
- codes of hierarchy (*li*).

Among these norms, 'codes of hierarchy' (*li*) is considered to be the core of this concept system. It suggests that everyone must confirm their status within a specific social rank. The upper class requires that lower-status classes demonstrate loyalty to them. On the other hand, lower-status classes expect that people of high status show kindness in response to their loyalty. All Confucian principles are based on hierarchy. Collectivism, or interdependence, is built upon a hierarchical social framework. Respect for tradition requires that everyone follow norms and values as stipulated by elders or people in authority. 'Face protection' ensures that everyone is sensitive to each other's hierarchical status. Essentially, the basic differentiation between Chinese and Western cultural values originates in this dynamic.

Collectivism

In Chinese culture, collectivism defines individual status. Individuals are not identified by independent status as such, but by dependent relations within the hierarchical system. Confucianism emphasises the importance of maintaining harmonious interpersonal relationships. In meeting this requirement a person should act in accordance with external expectations rather than with their own internal wishes or desires. Traditional national values maintain that any intention of independence, such as competition with or distinction from others, is self-seeking and destructive. It is in fact considered selfish and immoral.

In a wider cultural sense, traditional Chinese concepts of collectivism mean that a 'one-man' or 'one-woman' domination system prevails. In this system the person at the summit of the hierarchical scale possesses absolute authority, with everyone under that assuming a level of dependence on their superior authority. Giving up individual interests in favour of a higher social prerogative is considered one of the character dimensions of a Confucian 'perfect personality'. The Confucian 'ethical man' is more than morally just—he or she is a cooperating member of society. Confucianism does not conceive of individuals as existing separately from the social structure, but as ethical components to a greater whole.

'Face Protection'

'Face' is a concept that is not held by Chinese people uniquely: it has universal applicability. The reason that it is more often identified as a Chinese or Asian value is that it is more important to the cohesion of a collective society like China than it is to the more individualistic societies of the Western world. There are numerous common expressions about 'face' in Chinese culture, including 'losing face', 'hurting face', 'protecting face', 'giving face' (elevating someone's self-esteem as ell as their esteedm in the eyes of others), 'wanting face' (desiring esteem within relationships), 'struggling for face' and 'having face'. In all of these expressions 'face' represents prestige and respect.

The concept of 'protecting face' contains a twofold meaning. When something affects the relationship between people, one side wants to protect his or her own personal standing, and simultaneously also wants to protect the prestige of others involved in the relationship. Consequently 'face' deals with relationships between one's own status or image and public acceptance; between one's and another's reciprocal obligations; and finally between oneself and people of a higher or lower social scale. When something affects the individual's standing or reputation, then it has both 'upward' and 'downward' social ramifications; this applies equally to 'wanting face' or 'struggling for face' as it does to 'losing face'. All relationships, especially between friends, relatives or colleagues, are reciprocal. One must do one's best to reciprocate a 'favour'. The untoward consequence of social carelessness in not repaying a favour may be the 'loss of face'.

The concept of 'face protection' in Chinese culture is, like most aspects of Chinese society, associated with hierarchy. 'Face protection' emphasises that a person should meet superiors' social or personal requirements. In this process the individual is thus obliged to demonstrate unqualified cooperation after properly identifying themselves modestly within the terms of rank. From a Chinese point of view this value is a necessary condition for any individual to function appropriately within society and within their vocation. A person of lower relative social standing must be sensitive to the social requirements of those higher on the social scale. They must also be aware of the absolute importance of authority.

For example, a subordinate would assume that their boss had extended 'special face' if the boss requested a favour after work time. This request would be interpreted as meaning one of two things. First, that the boss trusted them more than others; and second, that the boss was closer to them than to other employees. In both cases the experience would be considered positive and even beneficial. Refusal to cooperate would hurt the boss's 'face' and may even bring about a negative result in the employee's career. A refusal of this type is not just a refusal of a favour per se, but the rejection of a relationship. 'Face protection' is an essential stitch in the rich tapestry of Chinese business culture. Its influence can be seen in every aspect of leadership style, customer psychology and negotiation strategy. These topics will be described in more detail in later chapters.

Respect for Tradition

Chinese people have a strong orientation towards the past. In traditional China, first-order preference is given to both the study of history and ancestor veneration. This means that the ideas of elders and predecessors are thought of as practically imperial edicts. The younger generation must follow regulations established by the 'aged', more often than not identified as the 'older generation'. In the veneration of elders, both the strength and weakness of the Chinese social system is revealed. In the first instance, authority is synonymous with tradition, and tradition then dictates automatic deference to hierarchy—a form of circular logic. In a positive sense, this approach has produced the longest continuous civilisation in human history. However, in this stability lies the Chinese social systems' greatest weakness: because deviant behaviour is not tolerated, ironclad mores lead to a debilitating incapacity to adapt, innovate or change, with the result that the Chinese adhere to convention in a similar way to the religious obligations of people in the monotheistic West. In traditional China this reluctance to change was practically a religious value. In recent years confusion over this respect for tradition has led to many grave misunderstandings between China and the West.

Misunderstandings about the notion of respect for tradition originate from differing ideas or perspectives about religion. Chinese people practise ancestor worship while most religious Western people are exclusive God-worshippers. This discordance in the object of worship results in a significant difference in people's mental programming. Exclusive God-worshipers believe that God is transcendent. This belief leads people to think that moral principles originate in the spirit world and that they are separate from the managerial principles in the worldly workplace. People holding this view easily accept a concept by which management formulates dynamic practical demands in the workplace rather than falling back on unchangeable traditional moral law. Ancestor-worshippers on the other hand believe that the younger generation should adore the family founder as the fount of moral authority.

The main characteristics of ancestor worship are that, first, the object of worship is based on the secular rather than on the supernatural world. Second, that ancestor worship is related to age and position in a family or social structure. And finally, it is believed that the heritage of moral law must be followed in worldly affairs once it has been established by the aged. The consequence of this world-view is that Chinese people venerate a secular authority that has a direct association with social standing and hierarchy.

It is significant then to mention that while Chinese ancestor veneration has weakened in recent years, the 'worship' of tradition (the extension of ancestor worship) still plays a major role in many organisations. Most elderly Chinese still believe that tradition cannot be and must not be neglected.

Egalitarianism

Egalitarianism is an important aspect of Confucianism. To the Chinese, however, it is very different from the same concept seen in Western culture. Chinese egalitarianism focuses on equal *result* rather than equal opportunity. Confucianism maintains that society would be more stable if wealth and income were allocated equally within one constant economic and social system. A Chinese proverb maintains 'Do not worry that people are poor, but rather be concerned if wealth is not allocated equally'. Actually, according to this interpretation, Chinese egalitarianism is a form of 'shared poverty'. According to Confucianism, people would accept their poverty and not challenge the political structure if they felt everybody was in equal economic standing within the same rank. This consciousness remains deeply embedded in Chinese culture, even to the present day. For example, most state-owned organisations in China maintain and continue to support salary categories for their employees within the principle of 'low income, small differences'.

Business Values of the Past

Confucianism has constituted the ideological engine of almost every aspect of Chinese society for more than 2000 years. It has profoundly contributed to the development of Chinese business culture.

Agriculture versus Commerce

China has always been an agrarian-based society. In agricultural societies almost all goods are produced for subsistence consumption, or for the payment of state taxes in kind. Generally speaking, Chinese governments right down through history have based most of their policies around support for agriculture, always at the expense of mercantile activities. The traditional Chinese value of attaching importance to agriculture and belittling commerce has retarded China's potential as a major trading nation for over 2000 years. Confucianism argues that the objective of state power is to maintain social stability. Agriculture is believed to be the base of stability because it restricts people to fixed geographical areas. Politically it makes people easier to govern and to control. Traditional Chinese rulers believed that the mobility of commercial activities could potentially undermine stability. Furthermore, commercial transactions can only result in individual benefit, not wealth for society in general. Consequently, the Chinese historically have a very poor appreciation of the principles of commodity exchange. Confucianism emphasises that a moral person should be concerned with righteousness and benevolence rather than with benefits.

This view discriminates against the accumulation of wealth by commerce. It requires Chinese businesspeople to place more emphasis on moral than on economic benefit, a sentiment that still exists in China's developing market economy. Many Chinese entrepreneurs in fact like to be seen to enthusiastically sponsor various benevolent or philanthropic public projects. 'Good publicity' or rather 'public relations' will establish a person's Confucian 'moral credentials' against allegations of individualistic profit-seeking.

From the beginning of Chinese civilisation until recent times, commerce has had to contend with these negative social values. In looking at this problem, what many foreign experts on China fail to point out in their search for a cultural theory is that China's place in history as a great trading nation has occurred in spite of this particular value, not because of it.

Business—Crafty and Unscrupulous

Clearly in the past Confucian culture has had a low regard for business in general. This is seen in the traditional hierarchical structure of Chinese society, which is largely ranked according to relative social value. According to Chinese tradition there are four social classes: officials and intellectuals, peasants, workers, and finally at the bottom of the heap, businessmen. The businessperson, ranked at the bottom of the society, is regarded by Confucianism as the 'mean man' (*xiao ren*). This is because

Confucianism stresses that the 'superior man' understands righteousness (*yi*), whereas the 'miserable man' merely comprehends benefits (*li*). A decent person focuses on kindness, while a base one focuses on personal profits or interests. Chinese tradition then generally regards the merchant as an unscrupulous person. This does not mean that Confucianism has not accommodated business into its moral code: in practice the purpose of commerce in China was to be found in the long-term enrichment and subsequent preservation of the family unit.

Before 1978 this traditional value strongly influenced Chinese people's belief that commerce was a base occupation. In traditional Chinese culture most Chinese intellectuals pursued careers as officials of the ruling class; a career in commerce was an imprudent career option. In traditional Chinese society, to engage in business was to invite contempt. 'Mind Liberalisation' and the benefits of China's Open Door policy have combined to weaken the influence of this view.

Limiting Personal Motive in the Pursuit of Wealth

Traditional Chinese values condemn self-actualisation and emphasise the non-individual elements of social organisation. Confucianism argues that all forms of self-promotion, such as exerting personality in the workplace, will cause people to compete in favour of their own selfish interests. Confucianism significantly regards selfishness as the root of all evil. So the accumulation of personal wealth by commerce—a form of selfishness—was in Chinese traditional society afforded a low priority.

At the time, peasants, who incidentally still make up the great mass of the Chinese population, upheld the virtue of 'being satisfied with things as they are'. The discouragement of competition actually existed in all aspects of Chinese social life, and the pursuit of wealth was limited by this view. This negative Confucian value was extensively promoted during the Cultural Revolution of 1966–76, during which time the Chinese government prohibited all forms of private enterprise, regarding business as the 'tail of capitalism which needs to be cut off'. For this reason, competitive commercial behaviour in contemporary China can only be dated back to 1978.

The Seamlessness of Business and Officialdom

We have shown that traditional Chinese business culture holds a negative view towards commerce and trade. However, in pre-modern, traditional China, business activities were still very much essential to the life of the nation, despite the influence of Confucianism. Hence in the history of China we see many examples of various governments attempting to control national commerce and trade in an attempt to impose 'balance'.

Throughout China's history until the present day, an unbroken government philosophy ensured that state officials controlled business with the objective of limiting business's alleged socially destabilising influence. Naturally, governmental officials involved in commerce used their privileged positions to guarantee business success. Gradually many came to accept that a 'seamless' relationship between business and bureaucracy was a successful way to conduct commerce.

In the history of China many governments have reinforced the value of a seamless relationship between business and bureaucracy by their trade policies. The Qing government, for instance, in enacting its Closed Door trade policy from 1757, dictated that only a select few officials could operate trade between China and the outside world, and that trade should be conducted out of a single location, Guang Zhou City. These officials represented the Qing government in all aspects of international trade, an action which established powerful monopolies across the entire spectrum of international trade.

Likewise, after the Communist Party of China (CCP) assumed office in 1949, foreign trade still came under the control of government. Ordinary enterprises were deemed to have no right to engage in international commerce. Only a select few governmental companies were permitted to engage in foreign trade. These companies specialised in the purchase of domestically produced agricultural and industrial products, which they then traded against foreign goods and services on the open market. In a sense it was back to the bad old days of the Qing Dynasty, when only a few governmental officials were permitted to deal directly with foreigners. This situation remained virtually unchanged until 1978.

Authorising qualified companies to deal in foreign trade was an important aspect of China's economic reform package. Currently, many large state-owned organisations, corporations, private companies and joint ventures have the right to deal with the West. The culturally sanctioned privilege of a few governmental companies, which until recently monopolised China's foreign trade, has been broken. Unfortunately the value of the seamless relationship between business and bureaucracy still impacts on the realities of today's Chinese business culture—most Chinese people in fact take it for granted that a successful business must have a close relationship with individual government officials. How Chinese culture interfaces with business in the context of a strong state system is the subject of Chapter 6.

Chapter Three

Modern Chinese Business Values and Behaviour

In the last chapter we argued that before 1978 some traditional Chinese values held back China's development of commerce and trade. However, what is beyond dispute is that this situation is changing rapidly. Deng Xiao Ping's Open Door policy has created the possibility of challenging many traditional cultural and economic assumptions. Perhaps this has partially been the result of foreign influence. Perhaps it has partly been a consequence of the global expansion of various forms of technology, including the electronic media. Many people believe that change is simply part of the evolution of a uniquely Chinese system of commerce. Nevertheless, the Chinese people recognise that economic and social reforms have brought real benefit. What is certain is that the Open Door experience has broadened the minds of Chinese businesspeople to new ways and new opportunities.

Business Fever

Business values in Chinese society have undergone profound change since 1978. More and more Chinese people now see a career in business as an acceptable vocation. Initially this led to what the Chinese press identified as 'business fever'. Particularly between 1979 and 1997, many Chinese people chose business as their best opportunity to make money. This situation was especially true of Chinese intellectuals, who now favour business as one of the best career options—many Chinese intellectuals have challenged the traditional value of study as a path to being an official. This cultural shift has been the subject of a great deal of public interest in China.

'Business fever' first emerged, or rather was identified, in 1984. At that time many employees of state-owned enterprises, rural peasants, university students and some intellectuals began to enter the emerging part-time job market. The second outbreak, which appeared in 1990, was characterised by the defection of governmental officials and university lecturers to the commercial sector. Many thousands of China's best and brightest put aside the 'iron rice bowl' of state job security in favour of an uncertain future in business.

'Business fever' had immediate and long-term ramifications. In the short term it meant a readjustment of salaries, conditions of employment and expectations as China's experiment with Deng-style reforms was tested for the first time. In the longer term it meant a profound change in the traditional belief patterns of ordinary Chinese people and intellectuals. 'Business fever' marked the beginning of the end for a 2000-year-old social value, namely, that officialdom was the natural destination of a scholarly journey. This constituted a complete role reversal. In less than one generation, Chinese intellectuals had shifted from their position as the gatekeepers of Confucian values to being some of China's greatest agents and advocates of social change. This accelerated the formulation and maturity of a modern business culture across the whole country. These modern Chinese business values can best be understood by examining the following.

The Desire for Profits

In the past, Confucian belief strongly suggested that the pursuit of profit was immoral. For obvious reasons this view has been repudiated by an emerging generation of Chinese businesspeople and enterprise managers. Chinese businesspeople now argue that profitable business per se is actually a means of ensuring the efficient, equitable and realistic use of physical and human resources—an acceptable expression of 'community'. An unproductive, or rather unprofitable, business is now considered a waste of resources. Therefore businesspeople defend the importance of their new role in ensuring the balance of society in its entirety. The change in this particular business value has meant that most Chinese people now accept that good business means a stronger, more confident and prosperous China, not merely an exercise in individual benefit.

This fundamental change in values has produced the belief that a commercial organisation deserves to fail if it cannot meet a number of basic expectations, including:

- an enterprise must benefit the entire community
- a business must produce a profit
- a particular enterprise must hold a competitive capacity in the market.

Clearly in a global economy, successful business must be competitive. Some Chinese now have a well-developed sense of competitive values. And while in the past many Chinese regarded these aspects of business as the shortcomings of capitalism, people's attitudes to business have now almost completely changed.

'Being Rich is Glorious'

The concepts of 'result-equal orientation' and 'non-self-pursuing wealth' are deeply rooted in Chinese culture. Casting back to the words of Confucius—'Don't worry that the people are poor, but rather be concerned if wealth is not equally allocated'—it is easy to see why in the past people held a hostile attitude towards business. Significantly, this sentiment was not consistent with one of the Open Door policy's most important reforms, which was to cautiously encourage the emergence of an affluent business class.

This particular reform policy has sent a clear and positive message to the educated and entrepreneurial class and has become a powerful motivator for engagement in commercial activity. Indeed, beyond the highest levels of government and bureaucracy, business is the most realistic means of achieving wealth. In this way the pursuit of riches is no longer openly condemned as a shameful activity, but rather encouraged as being in the best interests and development of the economy, and indeed the entire society.

The Importance of Efficiency

Chinese society is complex. In China people have been accustomed to inequality between different social classes. Yet, paradoxically, it is a society where people of the same social rank have traditionally insisted on absolute equality. Absolute, rather than relative, equality among people of the same class means priority has been given to equality rather than efficiency. China's recent economic reforms has redressed this older value by the application of a number of popular mission-statement-like slogans such as, 'Give priority to efficiency by giving consideration to equality', which has become the catch-cry of the emerging managerial class in China. What is most significant is that people have now come to accept that efficiency equals profit, and profit leads to wealth and opportunity for the nation as a whole.

'Business Succeeds on Amicability'

'Business succeeds on amicability' is a traditional value that has become a prominent feature of modern Chinese business culture. Amicability emphasises friendly cooperation as the basis for success. Chinese businesspeople strongly believe that in business friendships are more important than regulations or outcomes. Confucianism argues that if people can learn to trust each other, then laws and regulations would be practically unnecessary. It emphasises the role of moral principles instead of legal regulations. For Chinese businesspeople, 'good feelings' and trust have an actual commercial value. Under some circumstances, business will be conducted without a contract, as a friendship-building expertise. And of course many discussions, particularly with Chinese officials, are informal, non-contractual and friendly in nature. In China you will be offered many opportunities to develop friendships, and later you will be given an opportunity to reciprocate this kindness.

Chinese businesspeople go to great lengths to end discussions on a friendly note. There is a common expression which says, 'No deal this time, but friendship between two parties continues'. Friendship is pre-eminent for both business and personal purposes. The deal can always be made at another time. Generally speaking, then, modern-day Chinese businesspeople believe that commercial business is not a winner-takes-all contest, but rather a process that results in wins for both sides. Successful business does not depend on a choice between absolute gain and absolute loss.

Chinese businesspeople use the words '*tang sheng yi*', meaning 'talking business', whereas in the West we call it 'doing business'. This is because Chinese businesspeople believe that it is through friendly discussions, often over the dinner table, that harmony and trust are established. Failure to appreciate this will lead to the failure of any company, foreign or otherwise, in the Chinese market.

Ways of Conducting Business

Relationships Have Value
Based on these business principles, personal relationships play a pre-eminent role in Chinese business. In the commercial world, Chinese businesspeople pay a lot of attention to the establishment of extensive personal friendship networks. There are several practical reasons for this.

First, competition is fierce and resources are limited. There is a permanent shortage of raw materials for production, as well as limited intangible resources such as access to capital or permission to trade. In fact, almost all businesses in China must hold a specific licence, issued by a number of central or local governmental authorities. At any given time there are many applicants or users waiting for permission to use those resources. Whether you obtain permission depends on whether you have a good relationship with a relevant government department. For example, in China only some companies are permitted to involve themselves directly in import or export trade, and permission must first be obtained from a number of departments. Suppliers or officials must follow the regulations that govern applications in general. However, an official is often at liberty to assist a member of his or her network group in a particular matter by fast-tracking applications. Although such behaviour would be considered unethical in the West, where we value officials' ability to distance themselves personally from business dealings they are involved in as part of their work, such concepts are new to Chinese business culture—it will take many years to supplant two thousand years of practice based exclusively on 'who you know'.

Secondly, in most Chinese organisations the hierarchical values of Chinese culture lead to a less than democratic style of decision-making. Usually only a few empowered individuals make important decisions or binding agreements, so it is crucial to identify and quickly establish good relations with these key people. For example, a marketer will have great difficulty putting their goods on display in a prominent and successful downtown retail outlet if they are unable to establish a business relationship with a key person within the particular department store.

From the Chinese businessperson's perspective, these relationships hold a value that is considered superior to money. Chinese businesspeople regard business relationship networks as a commercial investment or a form of insurance. This is the main reason why Chinese businesspeople hold so many formal evening banquets or lavish expensive gifts on guests or dignitaries.

They are investing in their business's future. You may often find that a Chinese firm will allocate what seems a disproportionate amount of their budget and energy to the nurturing of important friendships. This is also why most prospective Chinese joint venture partners go to so much trouble to explain to their foreign counterparts the extent of their influence within a network, especially in respect to the bureaucracy.

The relationship network is usually based on the intuitive qualities of personal feeling and trust. If you have not established a relationship with crucial people or with the appropriate government departments, then your experience in China will be a frustrating one. You will almost certainly encounter innumerable obstacles. And in the end you will fail. However, on a positive note, Chinese businesspeople will commit themselves wholeheartedly to a project if they feel that there is friendship and trust between parties.

Some Westerners may find this notion rather scandalous. The Chinese do not. It is an important part of their value system to seek out relationships based on trust—this is simply the way things are done. You should not, indeed must not, see this as corrupt behaviour, but simply as an expression of an alternative world view.

The Official Seal

Western companies sign documents with an individual signature. In contrast, government or private sector contracts or important letters in China must be stamped with the organisational or company seal. Chinese businesspeople generally consider the company seal more credible than a personal signature. If a top-level document has a signature, but not a company seal, then its value and credibility are questioned. This is further evidence of Chinese group orientation, which emphasises collective rather than individual responsibility. The organisational stamp or company seal represents a formal type of collective responsibility for the decisions made in the documents, so that any individual signature, even the top manager's, cannot entirely represent the organisation. In this way the impact of an individual signature in Chinese business is limited; contracts are only considered valid if seals are affixed to both sides of the document. Foreign businesspeople must pay careful attention to this—this vital information could effectively protect your interests in the case of a legal dispute.

One final point on this matter is that a valid document may require the affixing of numerous seals. Due to the bureaucratic nature of the Chinese government, the affixing of seals often takes time. Chinese businesspeople make a joke of this long procedure by referring to it as 'official seal travelling'. Consider the fixing of seals as much ceremonial as legal.

Saying 'No' Indirectly

Western businesspeople easily say 'no' to their counterpart in refusing or rejecting an offer or compromise, especially if they think the offer is unacceptable. However Chinese businesspeople strongly avoid saying 'no' directly, although they may not agree with the terms or conditions on offer. Due to the strong value of 'face protection', Chinese businesspeople believe that directly saying 'no' to a partner or associate may engender hurt and therefore damage a valued friendship or network relationship. Chinese people generally believe that having to directly say 'no' embarrasses both parties. You will often hear the words 'the matter is under consideration' graciously mentioned around the negotiating table. This expression is code—it indicates, without offence, that your offer has been rejected or is incomplete.

The reluctance to directly say 'no' is not restricted to negotiations between counterparts, but also encompasses a wide range of relationships. Many Chinese maintain that it is better to say nothing than to say 'no', especially if they have to relay any sort of bad news. For instance, in China an unsuccessful applicant for employment will never receive notification that they have not been called to interview, whereas most Western companies have no trouble in providing this courtesy. This practice is reflected across the Chinese business world. Do not be surprised or insulted when you don't receive a response to your inquiry. Other means have to be found of addressing the problem, such as discussing the matter over the table at the ubiquitous formal banquet, or by using a formal gift presentation to make subtle inquiries.

Good Fortune in Business

Essentially, Confucianism does not accept the existence of ghosts or apparitions, but does believe in Heaven. Followers of Confucius believe that life is predestined. In ancient China an Emperor ruled by a heavenly mandate, and was referred to as the 'son' or 'daughter' of 'Heaven'. Actually, for Chinese individuals, believing in 'Heaven' means belief in fate, or rather fortune. A common Chinese saying is, 'People make plans but their successful implementation depends on Heaven'. This belief does not abrogate initiative; it means rather that a good plan depends on personal capacity, but its ultimate success is determined by factors that are sometimes beyond a person's control. The Chinese call this 'the willingness of Heaven'. Accordingly, many Chinese businesspeople put great stock in *feng shui* (roughly translated as atmosphere and orientation), lucky numbers and 'physiognomy' or personal appearance, as they are all believed to influence fate and fortune in commerce.

Feng shui is actually a form of superstition. It claims to be able to look into the future by examining the physical orientation of an environment. *Feng shui* practitioners believe that there is a relationship between the cosmos and earth, and that a positive or negative spirit influences every physical location. During the Cultural Revolution, fortune, good luck and *feng shui* were denounced as feudal remnants, but the Chinese Government now takes a more tolerant attitude towards a variety of religious beliefs or superstitions such as *feng shui*. The traditional values of good fortune and *feng shui* have gradually recovered their prominence in China. It is interesting that many overseas Chinese businesspeople are strongly influenced by traditional culture, including a fascination with 'good fortune', that is as far as it relates to their commercial activities. This in turn has influenced, or as some people unkindly suggest, reinfected, mainland China. Dong Jian-Huai, the Chief Executive of the Hong Kong Special Administrative Region, for instance, asked a *feng shui* master to identify the best place for his new office in Hong

Kong, indicating the respectability that *feng shui* once more holds. Currently, especially in the south, *feng shui* is a common practice in commercial activities. Businesspeople will ask a *feng shui* master to identify the orientation and location of buildings before deciding whether to invest in real estate or select a business office, because good *feng shui* means good fortune.

'Lucky' numbers are now again the most popular means of determining good fortune among Chinese businesspeople. As in the West, the number '13' is believed to be unlucky. The Chinese consider the number '4' also to be unlucky because it sounds like the Chinese word for 'death'. On the other hand, the numbers '6', '8' and '9' are thought to bring good luck. The number '8' is considered to betoken prosperity. 8 August 1988 was considered by many Chinese to be one of the 'luckiest days in human history', and it is estimated that on that day over a million Chinese couples were married.

The number '6' represents a 'smooth' life without trouble. Since the sound of the number '9' is like the Chinese expression for 'a long time', this number indicates growth without failure. Chinese businesspeople are always trying to choose these numbers and avoid the unlucky ones in their private and business lives. They will pay a high premium for 'lucky' phone numbers or car registration plates. In some Chinese cities, registered telephone numbers or car licence plates are sold by public auction . A telephone number, 87888, was recently sold for 129 000 *RMB yuan* (about $US16 000) at an auction in Hangchou in the Zhejiang Province.

The Chinese preoccupation with numbers affects almost every aspect of business practice. A date based on lucky numbers must be chosen for a new company opening. The office level number must coincide with an appropriate lucky number. Higher prices are offered for building levels 6, 8 or 9, particularly for apartments in downtown Beijing. There are no level 13s in many Chinese office buildings: after level 12 comes level 14. Likewise there are few Room 13s in hotels or offices buildings. The fascination with good fortune even goes so far as being a determinant of price: many luxury goods are priced by lucky numbers in order to attract customers. Even the date of advertising must be chosen according to a lucky number.

Finally, 'physiognomy', the practice of determining a person's character from their appearance, is common among Chinese businesspeople. They believe that kindness or treachery can be judged by observing a person's visage. They often take special precautions towards someone once their appearance is thought to be negative or unlucky.

Applying Stratagems in Business

The modern Chinese businessperson believes that commercial business is warfare by other means, and that the commercial field is really a field of battle. Winning battles in business is a serious pursuit. Chinese businesspeople deal with this situation by drawing on their vast historical experience of warfare, applying stratagems and tactics that were developed over a period of over 2000 years.

Chinese business strategies are far-reaching. Chinese business is an international exercise, because Chinese capital is a global phenomenon. Outposts of Chinese influence and mercantile wealth radiate from Mother China like the spokes of a wheel. Vancouver, San Francisco, Sydney, Surabaya, Semarang, Singapore, Kuala Lumpa and Hong Kong form a chain of Pacific Rim centres of Chinese power that strategically place China at their cultural and economic centre. It is through these far-flung branch offices that Chinese business has invested huge amounts of capital in the international market, while at the same time luring foreign companies and investment houses into China-based joint ventures.

For instance, in September 1996 the US Ministry of Finance announced that the Chinese government and some Chinese companies controlled by the Chinese government had to date purchased US$12.1 billion in American Treasury bonds. This is consistent with the strategic outlook of Chinese business. They take the battle to their enemies' territory. Due to China's involvement in the global economy, many Chinese businesspeople believe that to be successful in a competitive international environment one must first be an excellent strategist. They suppose that it is important to hold not only professional knowledge, but also imagination, wisdom, skill and strategy.

Chinese culture bristles with stratagems, skills and tactics for advantage in a wide range of battle-field situations. One of the best known is the 'Thirty-six Stratagems' of Sun Zi (or Sun Tzu as he is better known in the West). The author of this document was the most successful general in ancient Chinese history. His work is widely read by Chinese businesspeople and is considered as relevant today as it was when it was written in the 5th century BC.

The 'Thirty-six Stratagems' of Sun Zi

1   Make use of camouflage. Weaken your enemy's position by concealing your own machinations.
2   Be patient. Let your enemies make mistakes and become divided, then attack them aggressively while they are retreating.
3   Let someone else do your dirty work. Entrust another to sow distrust and discord in the camp of your enemy. Discover your enemy's plans and then use them to your advantage.
4   Be patient. Induce your enemies to use up their resources. Provoke them but do not attack until you have a clear advantage.
5   Wait until your enemy is defenceless, then attack.
6   Confuse your adversary by taking a variety of deceptive actions. Then attack.
7   Put up a false front. Mislead or bluff your adversaries. Attack when your enemy is confused.
8   Reveal only one strategy to your adversary at one time, but have a secret plan that will catch them off guard and give you an advantage.
9   When there is dissension in the ranks of your enemy, be patient. Allow them time to become even weaker, then attack.

10 Make your adversaries think you are their friend, then strike while their guard is down.

11 Let the enemy win where they are the strongest, but utilise your strongest forces to defeat them where they are weak.

12 Watch your enemy closely to discern any weakness then exploit that weakness to the fullest.

13 Find out everything possible about an adversary before taking any action. Then act quickly and decisively.

14 Conquer or use weaker opponents to achieve your goals.

15 Use various ruses to get your adversary into your territory on your terms.

16 Harass your enemies by repeated attacks and withdrawals. This will sap their strength and lower their morale. When they are weakened, attack in earnest.

17 Lull your enemies into thinking they are in good shape, and then spring a surprise attack.

18 Destroy or discredit the leader of your enemy, and then their followers will give up the battle.

19 Find your adversary's weakest point and keep plugging away at this point until they are drained of strength.

20 Take advantage of internal strife to further weaken and confuse your enemy, then attack quickly and decisively.

21 Avoid making your adversary suspicious by secretly manoeuvring to withdraw.

22 Show no mercy when you have an adversary at a disadvantage.

23 Conquer your neighbours first, then target distant adversaries.

24 Make yourself the protector of small states in order to guarantee their loyalty and co-operation.

25 Take clandestine action to disrupt the strength of your adversaries, then attack.

26 Threaten small states with destruction if they don't join you in bringing larger states to heel.

27 Mislead your enemies by making them think you are weak and foolish, then when their guard is down destroy them.

28 Entice your adversaries into a trap by pretending to be weak, then close ranks and destroy them.

29 Make your enemies think you are stronger than you really are, then take swift advantage of them before they discover the truth.

30 Treat your adversaries as guests, then exploit their weaknesses and destroy them.

31 Fix your adversary's leaders up with beautiful women. This will keep them occupied and demoralise their troops through envy, making their army vulnerable to your attack.

32 Play the injured bird. When your enemy relaxes, attack.

33 Spy on your enemies and feed their spies false information.

34 Contrive to injure yourself or have someone else injure you in order to gain the trust of your enemy then exploit that trust and destroy them.

35 Create plots to get your enemies to destroy each other.

36 Do not attempt to take on an enemy more powerful than yourself. Run away and live to fight another day.

Chapter Four

Chinese Negotiation Style

 Negotiation is a crucial aspect of any business culture. It is a contest. And potentially it can involve cultural conflict, especially if both negotiating parties have little or no appreciation of each other's style. There are many books available that offer Western readers general knowledge about negotiating skills in the context of Chinese business culture, but they often serve up information as understanding, which is not always the case. Negotiation is a skill that must be learnt and then applied.

In this chapter we introduce the topics of Chinese negotiation characteristics, the role of the banquet and the place of tactics in business.

Negotiation Characteristics

The fundamental difference between Chinese and Western negotiating protocol is that the Chinese emphasise both hierachical rank and 'face protection'. The Chinese maintain tight hierarchical control over the entire negotiating process. These cultural traits determine the form of Chinese negotiating style, the composition of the team, the roles of members within the negotiating group, the means of negotiating and the way of implementing results.

The Initial Stage of Negotiations
The negotiating team's different roles
The Chinese prefer to use a large negotiating team, especially when dealing with foreigners. Teams usually include technical members and administrators, but sometimes involve representatives of local, provincial or national authorities, especially if negotiations take place overseas. These officials may be included in negotiations because of their position within the hierarchy, or because their views may have some bearing on the final decision. Alternatively, they may simply be taking advantage of the opportunity to travel overseas.

The managerial system and hierarchical values of many Chinese organisations determine that people play the role of the negotiator and decision-maker for different reasons at different times. To deal effectively with a Chinese negotiating group it is important to identify the team's various members. For example, a Chinese negotiating group representing a state-owned organisation often comprises two parts:

- One part includes functional technicians or professionals who take responsibility for collecting technical information and provide the team with an assessment of the significance and feasibility of the other sides' offer. Chinese technical negotiators are active agents within actual discussions. They easily and freely communicate with their opposite number, but have no authority to make any substantive decisions. In the final analysis they merely submit their report or message to the person or persons at the top of the negotiating hierarchy for consideration.

- The second part of a typical state-owned organisation negotiating team is made up of representatives of commercial and other bureaucratic departments. These officials are responsible for handling price and shipment as well as other high-level issues such as equity and capital injection. This second group is considered to be the Chinese team's 'tough negotiators'.

However, the real decision-makers, the person or group of people who make the final decision on behalf of the Chinese side, may not appear at the negotiating table at all. They may be above and separate from the two parts of the active negotiating team. This super-group waits for negotiators to complete their assessment and then takes time to study the information, subsequently raising and preparing questions for a second round of talks. This super-group thus remotely controls the entire process.

In some instances the real decision-maker may be a member of the second part of the Chinese negotiating group. He or she will usually sit silently and appear to contribute nothing towards the joint meeting. Such an individual enjoys immense power behind the scenes, because Chinese hierarchical values mean that very senior managers should not be physically active in negotiations but instead exercise their strategic intellect. Senior Chinese managers argue that receiving reports from subordinates and giving commands not only strengthens their position, but also benefits the result of negotiations by obtaining time for reflection. These demarcated roles of negotiators and decision-makers in Chinese-style negotiating often means that the final decision takes longer than it would in the West. Westerners often interpret this as a delaying tactic, leading to frustration and resentment, especially on the part of the leader of a negotiating team from an individualist Western culture. Understanding the characteristics of Chinese negotiating strategy and appreciating the specific role, function and concerns of each person within the negotiating framework is an effective means of speeding up this process and ensuring a mutually satisfactory agreement. Being aware that an inefficient bureaucracy sometimes causes a deferment of the final decision also helps to explain delays.

However, the first challenge is to identify the actual decision-maker and gain direct access to this individual. This is a matter of determining just who is who, and there are four ways to do this.

- You can exchange a written list of members of both negotiating teams before the first joint meeting. Examining your Chinese counterparts' positions or formal titles on this list will indicate the team members' role. Alternatively, Chinese people often record their names in hierarchical order, with the name at the top being that of the most important person in the hierarchy.
- The order of formal introductions at the beginning of deliberations may indicate the relative rank of Chinese negotiators. Normally the Chinese like to arrange for an interpreter or an individual of lower rank to introduce team members, working downwards from the highest to the lowest ranked position. The person introduced first is always the most powerful member of the team.
- Observe the seating position of your Chinese opposite number around the negotiating or banquet table. This will confirm the intelligence you have already gathered, by either confirming or calling into question the relative position of each player. Typically the most senior Chinese negotiators sit at the centre of the negotiating table, with their assistants placed on either side in descending order of rank.
- It is important to scrutinise business cards as another means of determining the key negotiators, since they differentiate managers from technical people by title and qualifications. However, it is wise to treat any senior manager cautiously—they may or may not be the decision-maker. It is wise to initially consider all managers as decision-makers, at least in the first instance, especially if you cannot clearly identify their roles by other means.

On the other hand, the titles and positions of the members of your negotiating side should at least match or be of a higher position and standing than those of the Chinese team. The more senior the standing of members of the opposite side, the more the Chinese team will believe that their counterparts take them and their offer of business seriously.

Negotiations starting with interpersonal relationships
Rather than launching immediately into direct business discussions, Chinese negotiators will first wish to talk with their counterparts about a whole range of non-business related subjects. These may include broad and convivial discussions about culture, art, history or food customs, and will usually also involve friendly questions about social or personal life. The purpose of this is to judge whether an interpersonal relationship can be established between counterparts before negotiations begin. Chinese businesspeople have a great desire to demonstrate their respect for their counterparts as a means of establishing mutual credibility. This is a genuine attempt at establishing a friendship relationship; but it is also a strategy to maximise opportunities and to ensure the success of negotiations. Notwithstanding, all businesspeople are potentially capable of breaking promises or changing contracts. However, the Chinese believe that a strong personal relationship cannot easily be ruined or broken.

A personal relationship is considered to be absolutely necessary for good business practice. It is considered more reliable than contracts or laws, in that it guarantees the social and moral commitment of both sides to achieving a negotiated goal. According to Chinese business perceptions, there will always be unpredictable or difficult issues to solve during and after formal negotiations. The Chinese believe that the best way to deal with this is to secure a sincere commitment from both sides to work together. They believe that commitment is based on trust, and trust is built on firm relationships. The experience of domestic Chinese business reinforces this practice. The Chinese prefer to start with informal non-business discussions that they hope will lead to the establishment of friendships before the negotiations begin. Actually, Chinese negotiators make every effort to build up personal relationships from the very beginning of the negotiating process. These efforts often take the form of a variety of leisure activities such as evening banquets, receptions and ceremonies, attending cultural performances or sightseeing.

For Western business negotiators, the initial stage of building a personal relationship, including participation in a wide range of social and cultural activities, may appear to be a complete waste of time, money and energy. For many Western people this often convoluted ritual is too much to bear. Frustrated Westerners often rush to conclude outstanding issues in the vain hope that this will speed up a negotiated settlement.

Many Westerners are particularly task- and efficiency-oriented, and often see little need to attend to non-task-related topics in conversation with their Chinese counterpart. They usually want to come straight to the point. The individualist nature and formality of many Western legal systems supports this business practice. However, if negotiations are to be successful then task-orientated individuals will have to look at the benefits of adapting their strategy to complement, not clash with, Chinese negotiating style.

The Middle Stage of the Negotiating Process

When negotiations become more focused, the Chinese technological negotiators often act as messengers. They collect information but resist making statements about possible deals. They try to learn as much as possible about the other side's goals, advantages, disadvantages and interests, which they then report back to the real decision-makers within their organisation or company. In subsequent rounds of discussions, the Chinese team will negotiate according to the remote instructions of the decision-makers. The process will then be repeated as more information is collected for reporting again, often involving several rounds. The purpose of this is to establish an in-principle agreement about common goals. Discussions can then gradually become more detailed as various specifics are introduced into an evolving outcome.

This approach results from Chinese cultural values, the carefully defined role of negotiators, the hierarchical managerial system, and even tactical or strategic concerns. Chinese businesspeople like to digest information before they contemplate a decision. They then prefer to step back from the process and think over offers or speculate about perceived traps. This avoids uncertainty, as negotiations become more critical. In turn, everything must be reported back to higher management, and often to different departments or levels of administration. This maintains hierarchical power in the form of collective responsibility for the final decision.

In general, there is a definite advantage in learning as much as possible about cross-cultural ways of doing things. By playing the rules, Westerners can even beat the Chinese at their own game. By anticipating the next step in the process, you can pre-empt certain culturally motivated moves. Because Westerners are outside the Chinese cultural paradigm they are able to develop an outside-in view that puts negotiations into a cultural perspective. They can step back and with skill and confidence control the situation in the same way as the Chinese decision-makers do. This ultimately speeds up the entire process and prevents either side from seeking out a competitor because of misunderstanding or frustration. To achieve this position there are three principles to keep in mind.

Being patient
Obviously, for foreign businesspeople operating in China it is important to practise patience. Because of hierarchical social values, the peculiarities of the Chinese managerial system, a desire to develop friendships as well as tactical concerns, Chinese negotiators often prolong the negotiating process. Obviously foreign counterparts wish to reduce time-consuming activities where possible. However, be careful. Your Chinese counterpart may take advantage of your impatience, especially if you have exhibited anxiety about signing the contract because of time restraints or expense. You must be prepared to negotiate longer than you would otherwise like to. Meanwhile you can be looking for a reasonable excuse to justify truncating the negotiating time.

Leaving room for compromise or concession
Unlike other Asian negotiators, such as Koreans or Japanese (who strongly resist offering concessions during negotiations), Chinese negotiators like to bargain. They in fact see the offering of concessions at any time during negotiations as prudent practice (or as a negotiating strategy). This is true of both private business and government-owned enterprises. Chinese businesspeople see the offering of concessions as an important component of the overall process.

Negotiating objectives can be ranked as follows:

• What must be achieved
• What it is hoped will be achieved
• What is considered a desirable outcome.

Simultaneously, negotiators will constantly relate concessions to objectives in terms of what is to be conceded. This is further divided into two hypothetical positions:

• What constitutes a modest concession?
• What concession is the negotiating team least willing to concede? What is their bottom line position?

When a negotiator uses a 'most willing to concede' concession to gain an objective, this is regarded by the Chinese side as a win for both sides in the negotiations.

For many Western negotiators, compromise is generally regarded as a half-win, half-lose failure rather than a 'win–win' solution. This is because Westerners generally set the negotiable point too close to the bottom line at the beginning of the process. Chinese negotiators, however, generally use compromise as a major conflict resolution device, regarding it as an opportunity to manoeuvre towards a 'win–win' solution. The Chinese provide counterparts with a 'most willing to concede' concession at the negotiating table in the very beginning of the process, holding back other more delicate concessions, which they then offer as required. In other words, Chinese negotiators typically leave plenty of room for compromise within a possible range of settlement options. You must bargain first, and only then look for an agreement. The Chinese consider a counterpart who is not willing to bargain as less than genuinely interested in doing a deal, especially if there are few or no compromises offered along the way. Western negotiators who offer few or no compromises are considered by the Chinese as inflexible or insincere. The wisest and therefore most effective way of dealing with Chinese negotiators is to leave enough room for compromise at the beginning of the negotiating process and then proceed to an agreement by offering concessions.

Refraining from public shows of power, pressure or position
Inevitably there will be disagreement between sides during most negotiations. The question is, however, how do the parties involved settle the point and reach an agreement without losing substantial interests? There are many ways of addressing this problem. A Western negotiator may use whatever skills and strategies are available to handle disputes or disagreements. But one strategy common in the West which you must never use is pushing negotiations by exerting power or position to the extent that it will hurt your Chinese counterpart's 'face'. No matter how attractive a deal may be to them, many Chinese negotiators and decision-makers may terminate discussions if they feel that their 'face' is hurt.

Related to this are three possible reasons for a Chinese counterpart to call a premature end to negotiations. One is that many Chinese are sensitive about their public image owing to the high premium placed on 'face protection'. This may include potential or perceived affronts to their person, their company or their nation. The Chinese like to be respected, and they are proud of the success and achievements of their country. They insist on fair treatment in terms of their position within the hierarchy, and do not easily tolerate being looked down on, to the extent that under certain circumstances Chinese people see 'face protection' as more important than good business.

Another reason is that, because Chinese business culture is strongly influenced by the traditional value of collectivism, most Chinese are concerned with their relationship towards others and with others' feelings towards them. In turn, they expect to be treated similarly. This expectation, however, is not always realised in intercultural business practice. Because of advances in Western technology, management practice and even legal systems, some foreign businesspeople feel superior to their Chinese negotiating counterparts. Additionally, foreigners who are influenced by individualist values often take action based on their position, interests and feelings, without considering the impact on others. As a result, many Western businesspeople have little regard for Chinese custom or concern, placing a dangerously low premium on understanding cultural differences. This attitude may cause them to look down on their Chinese negotiating counterpart, presenting what the Chinese may identify as a superior air. Having said this, if you accidentally came across as a little supercilious on a single occasion, it is unlikely to substantially hurt the negotiation process. But on the other hand, if this attitude were to dominate the negotiating atmosphere, then the game might be over before it actually started. This is especially true if Chinese negotiators find that their foreign counterpart appears to repeatedly ignore their concerns or conveys the impression of despising them.

Finally, some Chinese negotiators, or their decision-makers, are representatives of state- or collective-owned enterprises or companies. The personnel management characteristics of these organisations ensures that issues of position and promotion are not always directly related to performance, but to hierarchy or to relative seniority within a particular organisation (although like everywhere employees who perform well are generally treated favourably). Negotiators may easily abandon what, for all intents and purposes, is a good deal if they feel insulted, as they believe that a successful outcome may not improve their standing with superiors or make a difference to their personal career. Alternatively, they may feel that a successful outcome will be too difficult to achieve, and halt negotiations for the same reasons.

You would be wise to take a great deal of trouble to nurture a sense of mutual respect through the establishment of sound personal friendships with Chinese negotiators and other relevant people. Ultimately this avoids disappointment, sudden cessation of discussions or substantive loss in the process of coming to a mutually satisfactory conclusion.

The Final Stage of the Negotiation Process

The most important point to make is that there is in fact no final stage in the Chinese negotiating process, even after the agreement has been signed, unlike in the West where negotiations are marked by a discrete beginning culminating in a non-negotiable contract. Chinese businesspeople like to negotiate contracts that offer reasonable benefit for both sides, believing that no one likes to participate in a business which causes anyone to 'lose face' and which does not ensure benefit for all participants—unlike the Japanese, for instance, who often aim for the best possible position irrespective of their counterpart's loss. For the Chinese, an ideal result is that neither side is seen as the big loser. Both sides must feel that negotiations have been fair and that the relationship will ultimately lead to solid business. However, sometimes serious misunderstandings occur after the so-called final stage of the negotiation process, Chinese negotiators consider the process to be completely open-ended. Indeed, many Western businesspeople complain that Chinese businesspeople continue to raise issues for further negotiation after an agreement has been signed.

This may be because Chinese and Western people see different meaning in the signing of an agreement or contract. For Westerners, signing a contract means that both sides have agreed to cooperate on fixed conditions that have only to be implemented. However, for Chinese people, the signed agreement merely marks the end of the initial stage of cooperation. Subsequent cooperation is contingent on the condition that supplementary negotiation may be required before, during or after implementation. Chinese businesspeople argue that there is no such thing as a contract without loopholes, and that there will always be problems that cannot be anticipated at the time of initial negotiations, especially for complicated or large-scale projects. Significantly, China's economic and social situation is at present subject to profound change and reform. Aware that the economic situation in China can lead to the failure of project cooperation with Western counterparts, Chinese negiotators naturally want to reduce this risk through supplementary negotiations after signing the contract. Consequently both Chinese and their foreign counterparts are becoming more flexible in respect to the cultural requirements of China's changing economic environment.

Another factor that helps explain this problem is that some Chinese businesspeople do not have a strong sense of the strict legal effectiveness of a contract or agreement. Since business relationships in China are based on personal feelings, these are considered more reliable than legal documentation. Many Chinese believe that although the main features of an agreement or contract must be observed, minor points can be subject to change, depending on the depth of trust or cooperative friendship relationships. Chinese businesspeople normally keep their word on implementing a contract, but they will continue to seek 'sub-concessions' or 'interpretations' on specific points, which they see as a means of securing more, not less, commitment to the agreement's stated goals.

Some Chinese businesspeople divide negotiations into two phases: signing an agreement of intention, and then agreeing to a contract. They believe that an agreement is less legally binding than a contract and only implies a basic intention to cooperate. According to their understanding, an agreement is subject to change in later bargaining. Hence Chinese businesspeople will sign an agreement in the first instance without hard bargaining, and will then use this as a foundation to construct a tough bargaining strategy that ultimately leads to the signing of a contract. Western businesspeople, however, regard an agreement as a legal document which, like a contract, is subject to fixed conditions.

This ambiguity is very frustrating for foreign negotiators. To reduce the potential for dispute, you should work with, and not against, your Chinese counterparts, carefully identifying the items within the contract that are for all intents and purposes beyond reasonable dispute. It is also necessary to explain and reaffirm with the Chinese negotiating side what is the exact nature of an agreement or contract before signing it. This takes patience and time, and is most effective if based on friendly relationships. Some foreign negotiators actually build into the agreement a mechanism for handling supplementary negotiations, so that no one is shocked or surprised when negotiations continue beyond the signing of a contract.

Terminating negotiations
According to the Chinese, an experienced negotiator avoids a confrontational stance that may threaten the success of present or future negotiations. Compared with Western negotiators, the Chinese use a less aggressive negotiating style. This is not to say that Chinese negotiators are less goal-oriented than their Western counterparts. The differences between them result from different cultures, due to the Chinese cultural values of 'business success based on amicability' and 'face protection'. An open dispute during negotiations is a danger signal; rather a sense of harmony is believed to be the foundation-stone of good business. Chinese businesspeople believe that harmony is contingent on the protection of one's 'face', and that aggressive behaviour in a public forum will hurt the 'face' of both sides. Invariably this results in both personal and professional damage. Consequently, Chinese negotiators avoid bitter or strong words, even though they may be unhappy or even upset about the substance or outcome of deliberations, and indeed may intend to terminate the meeting.

Chinese businesspeople avoid, practically at all costs, being involved in court proceedings or public arbitration. If this is inevitable, no matter what judgement results, they feel that the Chinese principle of 'no deal this time, but friendship is still important' has been betrayed, and that their organisation's public loss of 'face' will reflect poorly on their negotiating prowess. According to the Chinese, public confrontation announces that the cooperative relationship between parties based on trust and good feelings is over—the last thing anyone wants to see in a Chinese business relationship. By the time negotiations begin to break down, a great deal of time, effort and money has been invested in both friendships and networking. To their mind, open dispute creates a negative profile for both parties, and calls into question their capacity to cooperate with anyone. This in turn casts a shadow over both parties' authority in the business community. This can exert a sustained negative impact on their business with other companies or enterprises. In this way an open dispute leads to many lost opportunities.

If you are astute enough, you can ensure your business's long-term success by adopting the Chinese style of negotiation. This is an investment not just in the job at hand but also in profile and reputation. If negotiations have to be concluded prematurely, then both parties should take the opportunity to diplomatically suggest that the cessation is temporary. However frustrated you may feel, avoid throwing blame on the Chinese side or describing the negotiations as a failure; instead try to make the cancellation of dialogue smooth, positive and open-ended.

The Role of Banquets in the Negotiating Process

In China business is always related to eating. Practically every foreign businessperson who has visited or who is working in China has received an invitation to a formal banquet. For most Westerners their lasting impression of China is the variety, abundance and taste of lots of delicious food. There are many forms of banquets in China: a welcoming banquet, personal banquets, official banquets, company banquets and farewell banquets. Treating foreigners to a variety of generous banquets is sometimes interpreted by foreign businesspeople as a Chinese business tactic to soften up their foreign counterparts by making them feel important. Actually, the meaning or function of banquets in Chinese business culture cannot be explained in such a simple or negative way.

Banquets have both a positive and a negative role in business culture. This depends on how you perceive, understand and then make use of this important social activity. There are many stories about both good and bad banquets. Two notable and opposite perspectives include a foreign China-based managing director who was quoted as saying, 'They [Chinese businesspeople] eat and drink with you, then lie and cheat with a smile on their faces'. This businessman has been struggling for even modest success in China for over five years. In contrast, the manager of another company from the same country, in the same field of commerce, recently enjoyed one of the most lavish banquets of his long and successful career in Chinese business. This social event coincided with the signing of his company's 27th new business contract with a Chinese firm. An outstanding result!

Chinese Business Culture and Eating

The Chinese place a high premium on hospitality, and a popular way to show this is to lavish on guests a vast selection of alluring and delicious food and drink. Chinese cuisine is famous around the world. To the Chinese eating is a way of life. Enjoying food together plays an important role in making friends, reinforcing the goodwill between relatives, showing respect for seniors and celebrating festivals in the course of daily life.

No one knows exactly when eating became an integral part of Chinese business culture. However it can be said that one of the significant differences between Chinese and Western business cultures is in China eating is much more closely related to business than it is in the West. Eating and work are parts of the same process. In the West eating is more a recreational or social activity—it is something that happens after work. In China the two activities are integrated. Don't assume that Chinese businesspeople only treat foreigners to banquets in order to soften them up or to show hospitality merely to advance their immediate business interests. In effect, Chinese businesspeople treat every person who is relevant to their business as a special relation. Whether that person is an official, business counterpart, potential partner, top manager, expert authority, department head, customer or supplier, all could be guests at the same banquet table. As a consequence, the restaurant business has become one of the fastest-growing businesses in China since the Open Door reforms.

In every large and medium city in China, and especially those in Guangdong Province, businesspeople are eating and doing business. The cost incurred by the host is taken for granted as a necessary and essential business expense. For this reason the administration budget of most Chinese enterprises and organisations covers the expense of banquets. It may sound strange to foreigners, but eating is the heart and soul of Chinese business culture. There is little doubt that you must understand the role of the banquet in Chinese business if you are to succeed in the world's largest market.

The Roles of Banquets During Negotiation

Establishing a relationship

Banquets have four main functions in Chinese business culture. The first is in establishing an initial business relationship. For Chinese businesspeople the easiest way for strangers to get to know each other is to talk in a relaxed atmosphere. An ideal reason to get together for discussions is to hold a dinner party. At a banquet, both the host and guests can easily engage each other in topics of conversation as diverse as personal life, national culture and, of course, business. In the West we consider it somewhat unbusinesslike to talk too much about business at the dinner table—business is for meetings or for the boardroom. In contrast, business is usually the main topic of conversation at a formal banquet in China.

At a welcome banquet, Chinese businesspeople like to show their respect and hospitality to potential partners, and want to establish this relationship in good faith at the very beginning of negotiations. At the same time they wish to get a feel for the possibility or degree to which potential partners are willing to cooperate, and to assess their counterpart's personality or become familiar with their communication style. Chinese businesspeople strongly believe that this basic information will assist the course of future discussions. The welcome dinner, of course, could become a farewell dinner if the Chinese business host finds that there is no possibility of working together because of a lack of common interest or because of their counterpart's unpleasant personality.

Demonstrating a capacity to conduct business
Most successful negotiations in China are based on mutual trust, respect and confidence. Chinese businesspeople believe that the size, turnover, performance and assets of a particular enterprise or company are important elements of a successful business equation. They also believe that the banquet table is a reflection of this, but more importantly, of their financial power and political support. In order to instill confidence in potential partners, a particular Chinese businessperson first chooses the best restaurant, and then invites Chinese officials or other relevant important figures to join them. This, they believe, helps them build up a picture of their firm's credibility and connections.

However, at times the banquet table phenomenon has attracted the criticism of Western businesspeople who see the whole exercise as a costly waste of resources. The banquet table is not, however, about excess, or even primarily about Chinese food culture, but about the value of 'face protection' in Chinese society. This relates to the value of 'wanting face'—a desire to establish a sense of one's financial capacity through the medium of a splendid banquet; and 'to have face'—having the network to be able to invite important figures as dinner guests. Both the opulence of the table and the calibre of guests seek and illustrate 'face' in Chinese business culture.

Exploring the possibilities of further cooperation
Clearly most Chinese businesspeople prefer to discuss deals in an informal setting rather than in a formal meeting. In a sense they feel that the potential embarrassment of a public rejection represents an intolerable loss of 'face' and therefore take steps to make the whole process less formal and therefore less risky. For them, it is much safer to raise possibilities or broach demands through an informal or private occasion. Under these circumstances a Chinese counterpart may not feel a loss of 'face' even if their demands are rejected. The dinner table is in fact the ideal informal occasion to raise issues at hand, or, in a creative and relaxed brainstorming atmosphere, explore new opportunities.

Taking a break from negotiations
Conflict and argument in the negotiation process often lead to impasse, when neither side is likely to compromise. Once this occurs, the Chinese side may attempt to break the deadlock by holding a banquet to relax the tension of negotiations and give both sides an opportunity to evaluate their commitment to a deal. An invitation to dine during deadlock is a good sign—it indicates that negotiations are still viable. It also presents an opportunity to explore ways of circumventing the impasse.

The Time, Place and Means of Banqueting During Negotiations

Times and invited guests
Chinese businesspeople can treat their counterparts to a banquet at any time during the period of negotiations. How many banquets are held within the negotiating period depends on both the social status of the negotiating side and the success of discussions. If the rank of a Western counterpart is high, or they are perceived to be powerful, then the Chinese group coordinator will arrange as many banquets as necessary in order to explore the possibility of cooperation. The same would be true if negotiations were not proceeding smoothly. In this way the frequency of banquets is usually only an indication of the requirement for further intelligence gathering. Generally, however, there is at least one formal banquet, the welcome banquet. Possibly there will be a farewell banquet as well.

As part of Chinese banquet culture, guests are never required to pay. It is in fact an offence to offer. The same should also be true when a foreign counterpart hosts a banquet in return for their Chinese counterpart's hospitality. The Chinese cannot understand the practice of 'going Dutch' or asking guests to contribute to the cost of a meal in their honour. Avoid it, or risk being considered very stingy.

Sometimes invited guests are not directly relevant to the business at hand. They may be important players in terms of the potential opportunities they represent. Sometimes they are senior government officials. The Chinese like to use these special guests to indicate to their negotiating counterpart that they have high credibility and strong support. Simultaneously the invitation of special guests is an opportunity for them to strengthen the relationship with these important figures through their exposure to important foreigners.

Chinese banquet procedure

The Chinese prefer to allocate seating in terms of attendees' age or rank. The order of seating is best left to the Chinese partners' arrangements. It is considered impolite to select one's own seating without consulting the banquet host or hostess. At official banquets, the chief guest is often seated at the host's left. During the meal, chopsticks are used for all courses in Chinese restaurants. Don't feel embarrassed if you are are less than expert in their use, but dexterity and skill will cause heads to turn, particularly if you are able to pick up one, two or three roasted peanuts with chopsticks at once. Obviously trying chopsticks is a lot of fun, but it is wise to have a fork and spoon available as a back-up.

Normally the banquet formally starts with ritual toasting initiated by the host, who arranges for every glass to be charged and then toasts the entire group. A few courses later, after the first toast, it is expected that the principal guest will toast the entire group. Every toast is preceded by a chorus of 'Ganbei!' which means 'Drink up', 'Bottoms up', or 'Cheers'.

In addition, there are a number of other important aspects of Chinese dinner parties that you should be aware of. The first is that according to Chinese banquet etiquette it is the responsibility of the host or hostess to make sure that all guests are served the range of dishes on the menu continuously throughout the meal. A portion of each dish is first served to every guest and then made available for further helpings. In the West it is often the custom to consume as much of the individual portion as desired. However, according to the Chinese custom, a guest's plate is never permitted to be empty—as soon as it is empty it is replenished. We advise you not to leave your plate empty when you've had enough.

Alcohol is also part of Chinese banquet culture. The Chinese maintain that a banquet is not complete without it. Wine, beer and other drinks are provided, but some type of strong distilled spirit is often served as a basic standard. Many Chinese whiskies range in strength from 30 to 60 proof. If you are not accustomed to strong liquor, take care—Chinese liquor is very intoxicating and can quickly lead to raucous behaviour at the banquet table. If you're not sure you can handle it, take a sip and then claim that you can't drink powerful spirits, at least before the call to 'Bottoms up'. Otherwise, it will be assumed that you are capable of handling strong spirits and will be endlessly encouraged to toast the health of everyone involved. In some regions such as Beijing, Mongolia and Northeast China, hosts and guests can become completely inebriated without causing the slightest disgrace.

One example of a way in which inebriation can be used to advance the cause of good business comes from the personal experience of one of the authors of this book, Rob Goodfellow, who has been called to give many toasts at many banquets in China. On one particular occasion a very important Chinese businessman hosted the dinner. Mr Goodfellow was asked to toast this person many, many times. His response was, 'I would like to again toast the good health of Mr Huang. When I first toasted Mr Huang's good health he looked very well, but after three glasses of Chinese liquor Mr Huang looks three times better because I can now see three of him.'

A banquet is a merry occasion, characterised by a great deal of talk across the table. Chinese businesspeople regard the banquet as a celebration, not just an opportunity to eat. They do not appreciate a silent dinner guest, but enjoy a range of light-hearted conversation, punctuated by more focused discussions on a range of issues, including business.

Finally, it is a basic assumption on the part of the Chinese host that the foreign partner will hold at least one banquet in return for their counterpart's hospitality. If you don't arrange one your business relationship will not necessarily be damaged, but you risk being suspected of miserliness, or at worst, discourtesy. A common Chinese social value assumes that courtesy demands reciprocity.

Chinese Negotiating Tactics

Every business negotiator has their own tool bag of negotiating skills and strategies. Knowing more about the negotiating tools of your counterpart puts you in control. By way of analogy, Chinese businesspeople describe the commercial field as like a battlefield, in which the application of appropriate tactics determines the success or failure of a campaign. In the Chinese case, many of these tactics are drawn from traditional Chinese warfare stratagems, and every move is carefully planned in advance. Perhaps this is the reason why some foreigners comment that the Chinese treat negotiations like a war. Here are the tactics or tools frequently used by Chinese negotiators.

Knowing the strengths and weaknesses of the both sides

A prominent Chinese tactic maintains, 'Know yourself and know your enemy, and you may win one hundred victories in one hundred battles'. This means that you must first estimate your own weaknesses and strengths, and then evaluate these in the light of your enemies' shortcomings and succours. In this way you will easily plan a suitable and effective strategy against your rival.

A Chinese business negotiator tries to gather as much information about their adversary or counterpart as possible. Their preparation work is usually extensive, and involves everything from a detailed brief on their counterpart's business strengths and weaknesses to planning the configuration of the welcome banquet in order to maximise intelligence-gathering during the first cautious steps towards establishing a framework for discussions. The Chinese keep smiling as they listen intensely without saying much about any substantive issue, quietly processing this preliminary intelligence and incorporating it into their overall negotiating strategy.

Making use of vulnerabilities

Part of this intelligence-gathering involves identifying areas of weakness in the other side's position or personality. For example, if the Western negotiating side has given their Chinese counterpart the impression that they don't wish to spend too much time, money, or energy on lengthy negotiations, then some Chinese businesspeople may purposely arrange delays, thereby forestalling a final decision.

Ironically, Chinese negotiators sometimes use their own weaknesses to improve their position. They may try to get the other side to appreciate their particular problems first, and then take a great deal of trouble to praise the foreign company for being friendly, resourceful and powerful. Consequently Chinese negotiators argue that small concessions on the part of the Western company represent a friendly gesture that is perfectly consistent with their Western counterpart's high standing, and further argue that by conceding a particular point, the reputation of this foreign company will be promoted in China. However, it is important to realise that their claim may actually be true and not a strategy at all; it may be a genuine attempt to honestly convey the Chinese counterpart's lack of technological or financial power.

On the other hand, if this is a tactic it will be employed where the Chinese lack technological or financial strength and wish to benefit from their counterpart's experience without cost. The Chinese appreciate that Westerners like to talk about themselves, about their achievements and what distinguishes their enterprise as different and exceptional. The Chinese will listen patiently to this as they absorb relevant knowledge, advantage and disadvantage. If you understand this tactic and anticipate it, you should have no trouble in using it to your own advantage.

Using competitors as a weapon

One strategy that Chinese businesspeople often employ in negotiations is to make use of their counterpart's competitors as a means of persuading them to make concessions. Chinese businesspeople typically offer a number of hints that a competitor has been willing to provide a better offer. These hints become more brazen as the need arises, particularly if the Chinese side feels that negotiations have become deadlocked.

Chinese businesspeople may also suggest that the technology or products of their counterpart are excellent and further suggest that they prefer to deal with their counterpart over a competitor, but at the same time indicate that another company is willing to provide a better offer on the same item. This puts pressure on their counterpart to make the relevant previously refused concession. This is why in negotiation with the Chinese you must come to the table with a number of concessions or fallback positions. An intransigent bottom line position is ineffective.

Gaining a respite

During negotiations Chinese businesspeople are likely to employ the stratagem of requesting a respite to gather up more time to allow what they might call 'further progress', particularly if negotiations have degenerated into deadlock or have become wholly unfavourable to the Chinese side. There are two ways that the Chinese apply this tactic.

The first stratagem is represented by the Chinese expression 'red face and white face' (an expression taken from the masks denoting characters used in traditional Chinese opera), or what we would in the West call 'good guy and bad guy'. During negotiations one person plays a positive and supportive role—the 'red face'. On the other hand the 'white face' is the negotiator who appears to do things to undermine the issue at hand, appearing tough and uncompromising. These two people are actually working closely together.

There is a further strategy designed to gain time for the Chinese negotiating side, when a Chinese counterpart claims temporary inflexibility on the grounds that they do not have the authority to offer a particular concession, and at the same time the Chinese team indicates that their manager or other government official does have the right to do so and should be given the opportunity to carefully consider the matter at hand. In this case, Chinese negotiators are playing a role of a 'white face' while their managers are assuming the role of a 'red face'. Or in another situation, the role of 'red face' and 'white face' may appear to exchange opposing views between themselves and their higher management: the Chinese negotiators may say that they would like to concede to the other side's demand, but unfortunately their superiors do not agree with them, and then suggest that they need time to change their managers' minds. Nevertheless their purposes are the same, that is, to obtain time for respite or further intelligence-gathering. Sometimes what they are saying is true, and they genuinely do need to report, following the characteristics of the Chinese hierarchical system. But sometimes they are purely making use of it as a tactic.

Chinese businesspeople usually take their hospitality responsibilities very seriously, including arranging a variety of tour activities for their guests or negotiating 'opponents'. Again, like the banquet, these programmes provide respite when negotiations are not going well. Tours appear to be basically recreational and do provide respite; but for the Chinese side, business continues in an informal but effective way.

Controlling the final stage of the contest
The fourth of the 'Thirty-six Stratagems' of General Sun Zi is 'Be patient. Induce your enemies to use up their resources. Provoke them but do not attack until you have a clear advantage'. One side allows their rival to use up their resources such as time, energy and money. They lure their opponents to expose their strengths and weaknesses, and then fully ensure that they are in a superior position before assuming a more aggressive final assault.

The means for implementing this tactic vary depending on the situation. Chinese negotiators do not engage in exuberant debate, strong negotiating tactics, or bitter exchange at the beginning of the negotiating process. They may contrast irregularities in their counterpart's words or conditions, in particular between what they said in the early stages of negotiations and what they say towards the end of the process. This is designed to provoke a response, which may lead to a concession. In this case, they are employing what the Chinese refer to as 'hitting a rival's shield with his own spear'. They may raise an old issue, which has supposedly been already settled, but not fully accepted by the Chinese team, especially after protracted and unfruitful negotiations. They may suggest that these irregularities have unduly prolonged the process and that negotiations between the two sides must end because the time is urgent for making a final decision. As a result, they can push all the advantages they have accumulated in the last stage by a surprise move.

The important point is that in China, as in the West, negotiators can sometimes be too clever by half. If a particular tactic leads to an irreconcilable breakdown in what was otherwise a successful business partnership, then clearly the negotiating team did not have the necessary skills to navigate through to a mutually satisfactory conclusion. Whether the tactics outlined in this chapter work in business entirely depends upon how the practitioner applies them to a given situation. Indeed anyone is capable of undermining their business position in negotiations by not using the proper tactics in the most effective way.

There is no reason why, with patience and preparation, a Western negotiating team cannot exceed the culturally specific negotiating prowess of their Chinese counterparts. Paradoxically, this demonstration of acumen will strengthen business and friendship relationships rather than undermine them. The Chinese recognise and respect a worthy counterpart when they see one.

Chapter Five

Chinese Management Style

and Joint Venture Partnerships

At present more and more Western companies are entering the Chinese market with the intention of establishing formal business partnerships. In China successful joint ventures are usually those that have combined both Chinese and Western managerial models. On the other hand, the companies that have failed are usually those that have insisted on following their own particular management style and culture to the exclusion of the other. When cross-cultural conflict arises there is no effective management process in place to deal with misunderstanding and deadlock.

Practical knowledge of the general characteristics of Chinese corporate culture is essential for those foreign companies that want to conduct business successfully in China. This chapter introduces the characteristics of modern Chinese corporations and relates them to the main points of how to successfully establish a lasting and profitable joint venture agreement.

Current Chinese Corporate Culture

An interest in corporate culture has been fashionable in Chinese enterprise circles since the mid-1980s. Under the influence of Western management theorists and practitioners, a number of senior Chinese managers began to consider how they might construct their own uniquely contemporary Chinese corporate culture. These managers appreciated that this new model had to complement both China's traditional culture and the culture of its emerging competitive market economy. Since that time, a distinctive Chinese corporate identity has emerged. This now reflects both traditional Chinese culture and contemporary values in the context of rapid social, political and economic change.

Organisational Structure—'Two Carriages'

The greatest difference in organisational structure between most Chinese enterprises and all Western companies is that there are parallel management systems within a Chinese enterprise. One is an administrative system and the other is an internal leadership structure based around the Communist Party. Chinese managers often refer to this system as 'two carriages'. Before 1984, a Communist Party secretary controlled all Chinese enterprises, but after the 'Enterprise Reform' of 1984, a general manager was also made responsible for the overall management of these firms. Since this time both the Communist Party secretary and general manger has been required to exercise parallel responsibility.

Because of this the Communist Party is represented in almost every Chinese enterprise—state, collective enterprises and joint ventures. The main responsibilities of the Communist Party are supervising and guaranteeing the strategic direction of the enterprise and participating in important decisions, especially in respect to personnel. In some small enterprises the top senior managing director may be both the general manager and secretary of the Communist Party. However, different individuals hold the positions of general manager and Communist Party secretary in almost all large state-owned or joint venture enterprises. Because of the difficulties associated with operating a parallel system, differences of opinion often arise between the two management streams.

Organisational Functions— 'A Small Society'

One of the salient features of management in China is that organisations play an extensive role in both the professional and private lives of their employees. Most enterprises in China not only provide their employees with working opportunities and salaries, but must also offer a full array of material necessities, including medical insurance, housing, childcare, schooling and entertainment. Some large state-owned enterprises even provide their employees with on-site retail shopping.

The organisational functions of Chinese enterprises are like those of a small society. Most Chinese employees (at least those in state-owned enterprises) have a very clear idea that a credible enterprise must care for every aspect of its employees' life, including their work and family environment. Besides the usual development and operational concerns that all managers deal with, a Chinese general manager must spend a great deal of time and energy on dealing with employees' personal and private welfare. A credible managing director must be skilled at leading a managerial team that is responsible for a childcare centre, allocating limited housing resources, and organising the catering for special occasions and festivals. They are even expected to conciliate in a serious family or other interpersonal dispute. Clearly a senior Chinese enterprise manager's work is complex.

Actually, the employees of Chinese enterprises regard their organisation as a 'large family', in which the senior general manager assumes the role of 'parent'. Accordingly, managers receive the respect of employees normally afforded to the head of the family. In return, managers must take care of employees. If employees feel that their general manager has successfully assumed the role of a good 'parent', the particular enterprise will be cohesive and efficient. It will also be characterised by high employee morale. Employees consider managers who do not live up to this basic cultural expectation a failure, regardless of how profitable their company is. Hence, the mark of a good manager in China is not measured against management acumen and personal capacity alone: It is judged against whether he or she can secure basic material and welfare benefits for employees in the context of maintaining a high performance commercial enterprise.

In addition, the salary system of Chinese enterprises or other types of organisations is totally different from that of Western companies. In the first instance, employees are paid monthly instead of weekly or fortnightly. Second, salaries normally consist of four parts: a basic salary, seniority salary, bonus and subsidy. The contents of the subsidy component of the salary package varies across regions or organisations, but generally includes a subsidy for housing rental, medical care, non-staple foodstuffs, newspapers and books, transportation, even clothing and footwear. Beyond these items other goods and services are adjusted by each enterprise according to specific policy or performance. Every employee in a Chinese enterprise normally receives a monthly salary sheet that lists all salary subsidy deductions. Sometimes these items are so numerous that ordinary employees do not bother to calculate their total value. When you ask an employee of a state-owned organisation how much they earn every month, the figure they give you may be much higher than their official income. Only two salary items, the basic and seniority salary, can be easily calculated. The various other components of a Chinese employee's wage reflect the 'large family' principle which characterises most Chinese enterprises.

Corporate Values

Management in China is still deeply influenced by Confucian values, passed down from one generation to the next through family socialisation. Despite the Chinese Government's best attempt to negate the influence of Confucianism in the years from 1949 to 1977, its influence remains strong to this day. There are some common characteristics or management values that typify all Chinese enterprises, although as in the West corporate values vary according to each particular enterprise.

Management's 'impersonal achievement' orientation
Chinese managers insist on group or collective orientation. Requests for the recognition of individual accomplishment are usually denied. Any achievement by an individual is claimed on behalf of the group or organisation, although recent research indicates that Chinese employees' personal achievement motivation rating has become much stronger since the mid-1990s. As a consequence of this distinctive group or collective orientation, many Chinese managers adhere to a non-competitive management ethic. Only a type of 'friendly competition' between factories, workshops and individuals is encouraged.

This situation is very different from many Western organisations that are characterised by a spirit of self-actualising competition. On the other hand, the atmosphere in a Chinese organisation is less encouraging for outstanding individual achievers. Chinese managers believe that they must consider the feelings of superiors or colleagues who may not like someone who is thought to be trying to surpass them in the hierarchical scale. Chinese managers constantly try to strike a balance between modest individual virtues and prominence in a group. Chinese managers think that the ideal middle way is for everyone—subordinates, peers and superiors—to be qualified in their position and to be compatible with others rather than competitive. Chinese managers constantly express their view that individuals should work in harmony with others in an organisation and, for the sake of balance, should keep competitive behaviour to a degree that is acceptable by the majority.

Distrust within organisations
In many organisations, Chinese managers cannot entirely trust subordinates, partly as a result of hierarchical value. Chinese managers think of their enterprises as a family system. From a cultural point of view, within this system subordinates are treated like 'children' who must be dependent and cannot ever be fully trusted. On the other hand, the Chinese general manager is seen as a 'parent' who must look after and control his or her subordinate 'children'. Consequently, many Chinese enterprises are run exclusively by one powerful father figure. Since such managers consider that subordinates are not psychologically mature enough to take responsibility for managerial work, they make most substantive decisions on their own.

Cooperation based on obedience
Chinese managers operate within an essentially semi-authoritarian work environment. In this top-down system, subordinates are expected to yield to their managers and fully comply with their instructions. The conformity and obedience of subordinates is a basic cultural expectation and is therefore sometimes taken for granted by Chinese managers. Many Chinese managers believe that the relationship of cooperation in work, in which people assist each other to achieve work equality, should exist between employees at the same level. However, at the same time they strongly believe that an obedience relationship must exist between supervisor and subordinates. This is an expression of hierarchy, although in China this relationship is always referred to as 'cooperation'.

The importance of relationships and harmony
Chinese managers place a high value on informal relationships within an organisation. The Chinese word for informal relationships is *guanxi*, which can, however, also be translated as 'connections'. In some Chinese enterprises, unofficial channels or 'connections' are used to achieve organisational aims and objectives by the dispensing and repayment of favours or patronage. Because of this, compared with managers of other countries, Chinese managers often pay more attention to personal relationships within the work environment than to the job at hand. Chinese managers believe that maintaining good

relationships through all levels of an organisation is crucial. They are concerned with authority and power, but also use their position in a paternalistic manner to build up good faith and friendly working relationships with subordinates.

For Chinese managers in state-owned organisations, cooperation encompasses non-work activities as well. Managers go to a lot of trouble to establish and develop private friendships with work peers, superiors and directors beyond their work commitments. If possible they like to demonstrate their concern, or offer assistance to an employee on a personal or social level as well. The 'small society' characteristics of Chinese enterprises help to explain this situation, as does the fact that employees in state-owned enterprises normally enjoy a guarantee of lifetime employment. These characteristics force managers to concentrate on the establishment of non-work relationships to the extent that this is considered a prerequisite for maintaining sound workplace cooperation.

The Leadership Style of Chinese Organisations

Leadership or decision-making styles in China before the 1990s were essentially paternalistic or authoritarian in nature. During this time the delegation of power in most organisations was limited, with most of the decision-making power concentrated in the hands of one or two top managers or Communist Party officials. Recent years have shown signs of change. The degree of worker participation in decision-making has improved slightly with the introduction of a more consultative leadership style. This style has predominantly occurred in those firms which have accepted the consultant advice of outside professionals, especially those specialising in the implementation of consultative decision-making processes.

Formal participation systems

Theoretically, worker participation is one of the strong points of the Chinese management system. Unfortunately, in many enterprises theory and practice are two separate things. A system of formalised worker participation has been well established in China since the early 1950s, in the form of Worker's

Congresses (which are actually still in place). These officially sanctioned groups were authorised to scrutinise managerial work, to be involved in decision-making on various matters, and to air grievances or offer suggestions through representatives. Workers directly elected and still elect delegates to the Workers' Congresses. However the role of delegates is actually very modest: they are usually only permitted to participate in decisions related to working conditions, not strategic policy.

The role of middle managers in the decision-making process
Chinese middle managers are characterised by their deference to higher-placed authorities: they leave important decisions to a higher management level; they are unwilling to offer individual suggestions or opinions when requested to do so; and they are reluctant to recognise responsibility for enterprise performance. They are in fact trained not to make unilateral decisions. Most wait patiently for the single senior manager to decide on the correct course of action, and then carry out this manager's instructions obediently.

Identifying decision objectives through formal meetings
Chinese managers like to use formal group meetings to identify decision objectives. Apart from the Worker's Congresses, there is another legislated decision-making forum in Chinese enterprises: the 'regular working meeting with the Managing Director', which usually deals with everyday problems. Directors, heads of departments and first-line supervisors normally attend. Participation in these meetings is a formal requirement. The managing director usually dominates the meeting and others support his ideas. This is typical of the decision-making practice in state-owned organisations.

Collecting information and making final decisions
Because managers do not fully trust their subordinates, Chinese managers limit the scope of communication to collecting information themselves rather than from colleagues or subordinates. They believe that this is the most effective way of collecting information for decision-making. However, currently many Chinese organisations need to acquire urgent professional

...ledge from outside their respective organisations, and this has an impact on the style of collecting information.

In order to be competitive in the market, every Chinese enterprise must improve what they do and how they do it. With the increasing need for professional knowledge in every area of operations, Chinese managers are more aware than ever that decision-making power must be based on knowledge, skill and capacity. This is a type of new and positive authoritarianism. The old negative authoritarianism, based on organisational position or political background, only required a manager to comply with a superior's immediate demands. In modern Chinese management circles this attitude is fast becoming obsolete. This new authoritarianism is still related to centralised control within the organisational structure, but it can, with caution, be challenged through the knowledge and capacity of subordinates.

Chinese managers' preference for information from experts is designed to compensate for their own professional shortcomings in experience or knowledge. This gradual acceptance of expert knowledge is seen in changes to wage categories—professionals now receive much higher wages in comparison to ordinary employees. Clearly in China the concept of highly regarding expert technological or organisational knowledge is gradually being accepted as a social and organisational value, at least at middle and senior management level.

However, despite many positive changes in some negative organisational attitudes, senior Chinese managers still adopt an autocratic style as far as making a significant final decision. Chinese middle managers still have no substantial power to influence final decisions.

Responsibility for the implementation of decisions
Chinese managers, while liking to make decisions autocratically, believe that the responsibility for implementing decisions should *not* be taken individually. Although many managers say that they want to share responsibility between top management and colleagues, in their own minds the concept of 'management

as a whole' does not extend to the decision-makers themselv
This view leads to the tendency of Chinese *middle* managers .J
shirk responsibility whenever possible. Psychology suggests
that if a manager expected others to take responsibility, then essentially nobody would be in a responsible position, since the
question of who should take final responsibility would never
clarified. This apparent contradiction is seen as a virtue.

The question of who makes decisions and who takes responsibility for the decision-making process in Chinese enterprises
embodies two paradoxes. The first, which provides an excuse
for the second, is that collective decision-making exists in form
but not in substance, especially when a decision is made at organisational or departmental level. Although there are formal
participation systems for ensuring that management makes decisions collectively, many *top* Chinese managers, on the other
hand, still prefer to make decisions individually in accordance
with their particular position in the hierarchy. They often play a
dominant role in 'consultative' meetings, which in theory are
integral to the decision-making process, but are in effect a centralised decision-making process concealed by a mask of
collectivism.

The second paradox is that managers go through the motions of
taking responsibility, but actually make 'non-responsibility' the
essence of decision implementation. Most Chinese managers
are likely to avoid responsibility when an unexpected problem
arises. They are in effect culturally conditioned not to make final decisions (and not to implement the decisions they don't
make). Fortunately for them, since collective decision-making
procedure provides a convenient means of evading responsibility, managers can use collectivism as a pretext for escaping their
own individual management duties, since most decisions are
really made collectively through formal consultative meetings
that involve little substantial consultation.

The establishment of a modern marketing system, believed by
most Chinese managers to be a positive reform, confronts Chinese enterprises with competition. Whether the enterprise is
state-owned, a collective or privately owned, all must attempt to

increase productivity in order to survive in a competitive environment. Individual responsibility for work, individual incentive and challenges to negative authority in management are like new tools to be gradually introduced into the mechanism of management. External forces of reform coerce Chinese managers into reconsidering their managerial values and decision-making style. These pressures have actually led to progressive management reform, particularly in the areas of showing personality and capacity in management decisions, taking a competitive approach to business, and sharing power with subordinates in the final decision.

Although the 'one-man system' in Chinese organisations is autocratic, the style of management is changing. Managers' power now depends on their capacity to perform, and also on how they apply their professional knowledge rather than on their authorised position alone. The greater the expert power and knowledge managers have, the more support and cooperation subordinates provide them with in the decision-making process.

Joint Ventures: From Culture Shock to Managerial-style Mixing

Currently, there are three types of foreign businesses in China:

- the sole foreign investment
- the joint venture
- the foreign-owned and operated factory firm (which typically imports raw material for production and then markets goods abroad).

Chinese government statistics indicate that the establishment and development of these three types of venture in China have been dramatic. In 1982 there were 282 foreign manufacturing ventures operating in China, employing some 78 000 people. By 1995 the number had reached 59 311 firms, an increase of 200 times in 13 years. The gross industrial product of joint foreign–Chinese ventures in 1985 was US$2.71 billion, increasing to US$1202.11 billion by 1995, an increase of 500%.

Furthermore, as we remarked in Chapter 1, between 1980 and 1997 the Chinese government approved 300 000 discrete foreign investment projects, with a staggering total actual foreign investment of US$212.2 billion.

The rapid increase in joint venture partnerships in China in the past 10 years would appear to be an indication that China both welcomes and needs foreign investment. This may lead many foreign investors to assume that it is relatively simple to succeed in the Chinese market. This is not strictly accurate. Business reality in China is not always that simple. Many foreign businesspeople become successful only after first experiencing a great deal of frustration in dealing with their Chinese counterparts or encountering unanticipated risk factors. As a matter of fact, whether a joint venture in China is successful or not almost entirely depends on the foreigners' capacity to adapt to Chinese business culture. The process of establishing and promoting a joint venture in China is one of culture shock. Ultimately it involves the mixing of two styles of management, Western and Chinese. The alternate is unmitigated failure. The fact that Chinese corporate culture is so different from the corporate culture of other countries has an impact on the management of all joint ventures. In addition, the sheer magnitude of China's market and the complexities of its political, legal and economic systems is disorientating for first-time foreign investors.

These economic and cultural risk factors can cause many difficulties for foreign businesspeople in China, especially if they are not clearly and tactfully anticipated. In other words, to be a successful foreign investor in China, you first need to understand the differences between yourself and your Chinese partners, and then prepare to effectively overcome such difficulties.

Finding a Good Partner and Establishing a Joint Venture

First of all, as a foreign investor you must decide what you require of a potential Chinese partner to achieve your corporate objectives and goals. Then you need to answer the following important questions:

- Is the Chinese joint venture partner an entity enjoying full registered legal status under Chinese law?
- What is its type of ownership: state, collective, private or township-owned? There are different advantages and disadvantages in dealing with each of these different types of enterprises.

State ownership
Generally speaking, the large state-owned enterprises have the advantage of an abundance of skilled workers, a certain degree of technology and the support of the government. But they have the disadvantage of low effectiveness, a poor sense of market orientation and the heavy financial burden of employees' welfare provisions.

Collective ownership
Collective-owned enterprises have the advantages of organisational flexibility combined with a good appreciation of market orientation, together with a relatively high degree of production effectiveness. The disadvantages of collective enterprises are that they enjoy less direct government support, and the workers' qualities, the level of technology and overall performance vary from one organisation to the next. The final consideration concerns just how the particular collective enterprise deals with the government and with suppliers. Relationships are not always cordial, and need to be thoroughly investigated as part of the overall preparation towards making the right decision about a suitable joint venture partner.

Private ownership
Privately owned enterprises have the advantage of relatively high effectiveness. They are also generally free from bureaucratic interference. This group has the flexibility to hire and fire staff, and they possess a strong sense of a marketing orientation. Finally, they do not have the financial burden of having to uphold a comprehensive employees' welfare program. However, cooperating with this type of enterprise could be more risky than dealing with a state-owned organisation. At times privately owned organisations in China may have trouble obtaining the

necessary operational resources for production, because success in this area depends entirely on the personal relationship the senior manager or managers have with both the suppliers and the relevant governmental departments.

Town or village ownership
Township or village enterprises possess similar advantages and disadvantages to those of the collective or privately owned organisations. Additionally, they usually run their operations at a very low labour cost, although this may also constitute a disadvantage when you take into account the cost and necessity for training. There may also be problems associated with the potential for a foreign partner to be drawn into village-based local conflicts based on land use.

If the selected potential partner is a government-owned enterprise, you need to find out what government rank this enterprise enjoys. It may be connected to the state, to the province or to local or city government. It is important to determine this because different levels of government control different enterprise authorities. You also need to find out the professional capacity of your Chinese counterparts. How much power does your partner have to obtain supplies and raw materials? Do they have the capacity to assimilate a foreign technology package?

Finally, you must thoroughly investigate the financial capacity of the Chinese side, especially if it is a state-owned enterprise. Such enterprises sometimes have heavy financial burdens, even liabilities, as a result of their traditionally low performance combined with the pressure to compete, or because of the expense associated with employee and retired employee welfare packages.

Joint Venture Approval and Governmental Support

Obtaining government approval and support is another crucial factor in ensuring the success of a joint venture in China. A joint venture cannot be set up without government approval, and cannot effectively run as a profitable business without official support.

The State Council and appropriate provincial and local authorities are responsible for processing applications for permission to register a joint venture if the Chinese partner is a large state-owned enterprise or is controlled by a provincial authority. At present, the Chinese Government also requires that any joint venture project with a capital investment of over US$10 million, which intends to operate in the relatively well-developed eastern region of China, must first be approved by the State Council. In order to encourage foreigners to invest in the midwest of China, the State Council drew up a new policy in July 1996 which stipulated that joint ventures under US$30 million capital investment in China's underdeveloped regions need only be approved at provincial government level. In addition, according to government policy, the amount of foreign capital investment for any joint venture must not be less than 25% of overall capitalisation, with a further stipulation that 70% of joint ventures' products must be exported abroad.

Joint venture approval

Normally, there are four steps to achieving approval to establish a joint venture in China:

1. The first step is for the Chinese partner to present a proposal to the appropriate government agency. This proposal must include the type and amount of investment involved, the major products, the scale of operations of the joint venture, and the proposed duration of the enterprise. The foreign partner is also required to provide certain information to the appropriate government departments: its registered name, country of origin and legal address, as well as a certificate of accounting credit and a detailed explanation of the proposed scale of operations.

2. The second step is a feasibility study. This normally includes the economic significance of the investment, market demand, an estimation of the required necessary resources and raw materials, proposed project location, proposed factory conditions, environment protection measures and a projection of what number of workers and staff the proposed project will require.

3   After approval of the proposal and feasibility study, the foreign and Chinese counterparts can begin to draft the joint venture agreement. This agreement is considered a legal document, and must be in both Chinese and the language of the foreign partner. It should state the obligations and rights of both sides. One problem at this stage is how to decide the contribution made to the joint venture by each partner. Normally the Chinese side would hope that the foreign partner's contribution would be at least a large sum of foreign direct investment and technology (the two items that the Chinese normally do not have). On the other hand, the Chinese partner will be able to contribute most non-cash items, such as land, existing buildings, equipment or office utilities. You must assess these needs carefully.

4   Once the contract is signed, the Chinese side petitions the Administration Bureau of Industry and Commerce for an operating licence. Upon the granting of this licence, the joint venture is registered with the Chinese Tax Bureau and Customs office and issued with a banking certificate recording the proposed amount of investment capital involved in the project.

With the completion of all these activities the enterprise is officially recognised. Generally speaking, a contract which has been approved by the government is considered legal and binding. The Chinese Government will therefore supervise all aspects of its implementation.

Government support

Although the registered joint venture has the autonomy to control its own management and operations, there are many issues directly related to the government. Recruitment of staff, obtaining a bank loan, the purchasing of scarce raw materials, transportation, telecommunications and even water and electricity supplies, are all important operational considerations which involve the direct involvement of government. Both the foreign and Chinese partners of the joint venture must make every effort to secure governmental support at these levels. How to deal successfully with officials is the subject of Chapter 6.

Recruiting Suitable Chinese Employees

One of the keys to success in any venture in China is people. China's current labour policy provides the opportunity for foreign partners to freely select the best-qualified employees for their joint venture or offices with a minimum amount of interference from the state. Before the Open Door reforms, everyone in China had their job pre-arranged by the government after reaching working age or following graduation from secondary school or university. This was especially true for anyone who held an undergraduate or higher degree, who were carefully allocated a vocation consistent with the government's centralised labour market planning. One of the most important changes that followed the Open Door reforms was that both people and government now accept the idea that labour is a commodity with a value that can be exchanged in the market. This idea has had a strong impact on people's work-related values, and many Chinese people have now realised that they can freely choose their preferred job according to the market value of their skills and experience. This view has challenged the system of state-guaranteed lifetime employment, often referred to as the 'iron rice bowl'.

The selection process

Normally, there are five formal ways of selecting employees for a new joint venture in China:

- The Chinese partner may provide staff already familiar with the relevant field.
- By using the services of a government-based personnel exchange and service centre. These centres exist in almost every city or province in China, most being government-sponsored. They keep personnel files on individuals, and can organise personnel exchange negotiations and provide information on job opportunities for both applicants and employers.
- Through regular conferences with the Personnel Exchange. Government departments or private companies also sponsor these initiatives. Organisations include the China State Education Commission and the Provincial Education Commis-

sion. They hold extensive seminars for both job seekers and job providers, particularly for final year university students, usually each April or May. A variety of enterprises and organisations fulfil their recruitment needs through such meetings.

- Through newspaper advertisements. This means has recently become an acceptable and effective method of attracting key employees. The advertising fee varies between different newspapers as it does anywhere; the more popular the paper, the higher the fee. For example, a paper like *The Beijing Evening* is the preferred publication for recruitment advertisements because of its popularity with Beijing's residents. As a result, the price of recruitment advertisements in this paper is very high, and once the advertisment has been lodged it takes two or three months to appear.
- Using the services of a head-hunting company. These firms specialise in attracting high quality, specially trained professions. Their staff are usually proficient in English and have a rich knowledge of the Chinese job market, joint venture operations and the special needs of foreign firms. Naturally this service is more expensive than other options, but may be more effective in attracting senior executive staff.

Key points in appointing new employees

You need to keep a number of things in mind when recruiting Chinese employees. The first is that although it is not difficult for a joint venture company to recruit ordinary skilled workers in China, it is more difficult to recruit highly qualified staff such as managers in marketing, corporation law, financial, general or human resources management. And while there are many skilled and experienced workers in the labour markets of middle-sized and large Chinese cities, there is an acute shortage of professionals.

Before 1986, China's educational system provided few management development opportunities. For example, there was no MBA degree offered in China until the early 1990s. Because of this, graduates of MBA or other managerial professional courses have been heavily targeted by many of China's largest private or foreign companies. At present an MBA degree is very popular among young people, but it has been unable to go anywhere near meeting the present specialised employment demand generated by China's rapid economic development.

It is often difficult to persuade some top Chinese managers trained in state-owned enterprises to recruit marketing, financial or general joint venture management professionals. These old school managers have not realised the important role of professionals in running a market-orientated organisation. They are strongly influenced by the philosophy of a centralised planned economy. These managers do not have a well-developed sense of competition and management effectiveness, but are rather concerned with product quantity issues or the state-planning index for their particular enterprise.

The second thing to remember is that local governments in every large Chinese city have their own regulations related to recruitment of people from other provinces. Workers from other areas can be recruited to a distant joint venture only when they have been granted a Location Employment Licence. The Bureau of Labour in these cities issues these licences to local workers. The purpose of these regulations is to protect local employment opportunities.

The third point relates to a government regulation concerning the recruitment of senior Chinese managers by foreign companies or representative offices. This type of recruitment must be approved by the relevant government organisation (in Beijing and Shanghai the Service for Foreign Enterprises Company). The personnel recruitment details of each new employee, including employer provisions, must be officially recorded. The Chinese partners in joint ventures and foreign companies must both pay a service fee to register. To avoid this expense and further administrative trouble, some joint venture employers recruit their managers through informal channels, such as by the recommendation or introduction of a business colleague or by a member of a professional network. However, you must be aware that this is illegal in China and subject to criminal prosecution.

Fourthly, in China companies normally do not display the salary related to the advertised position in recruitment advertisements. This is usually negotiable on application.

A final important point is to be patient and flexible when looking for high-quality personnel. Remember that as a result of China's cultural values, its economic and political system is bureaucratic and complicated. Without the support and assistance of government officials, business cannot run smoothly or at all.

The concept of what constitutes a qualified senior manager in China may be totally different from that of many Western countries. According to the standard of most Western businesspeople, a person who possesses knowledge of the market or a particular field of technology, finance or effective sales and promotion strategies can become an effective marketing or general manager. Unfortunately, such people may fail as managers if they are not able to forge a relationship between the joint venture and the Chinese bureaucracy. Finding a confident and skilled manger who has experience in dealing with the bureaucracy, who is efficient and trustworthy and who holds a high degree of professional knowledge is crucial to the long-term success of any joint venture. Regrettably, given the acute shortage of trained managers in China at present, finding this type of person often takes a great deal of time and effort.

Ongoing Management of Joint Ventures in China

A successful joint venture in China must first recruit the right employees. You should then be prepared to 'mould' your staff according to your particular needs—the unique characteristics of the managerial system and leadership style in Chinese enterprises make this absolutely necessary. It is also, interestingly enough, a basic expectation of China's new generation of professional managers that they will benefit from exposure to Western modes of management.

How to Cope with the Communist Party within a Joint Venture

Most joint ventures have an operational branch of the Communist Party working within the overall structure. Operations are different from enterprises wholly owned by Chinese interests. The Party's joint venture branch takes a very low public profile. Communist Party activities are generally not held openly in work time. Usually cadres will not divulge their hierarchical status to foreign partners.

You need have no anxiety about the activities of the Communist Party in your joint venture. It normally plays a dominant role in most aspects of personnel management. If you are able to establish a good relationship with your particular workplace branch of the Party, then cadres, or workplace officers of the Party, can prove to be very constructive in their efforts to ensure that operations run smoothly and the joint venture is a complete success. Clearly the good performance of a joint venture reflects favourably on the Communist Party as well as the non-Party management stream.

How to Deal with Senior Managers

Because of their respect for hierarchy, age and 'face protection', Chinese older managers are very sensitive to others' attitudes toward them. They like to be respected. The best way to show respect is to consult with these senior managers in almost every decision the joint venture makes. You can achieve this by ensuring they attend a variety of outside meetings on behalf of the joint venture (although it must be remembered that many older managers have a poor command of English and little experience in technology or modern management techniques.

Most of these older managers are accustomed to an autocratic leadership style. They like their subordinates to 'cooperate' without question. Ultimately they prefer subordinates to accept their suggestions without participating in the decision-making process, in order to protect their 'face'. If you do not handle this diplomatically, then they may become obstructionist and undermine effective management practice. However, most of them do have respect for professionals and foreigners, and they may easily be converted into critical advocates of effective management. When you show that you respect their position and at the same time appear as an expert or professional in front of them, they will be keen to accept progressive management and work closely with you to achieve it.

How to Deal with Chinese Middle Managers

Most Chinese middle managers, accustomed to a work style of minimal participation in their original state-owned organisations, inevitably apply this style to their joint venture experience. The experience of many operating joint ventures is that Chinese middle managers do not participate positively in the decision-making process and do not like taking responsibility for any stage in the operations. They often keep silent when their personal opinions are sought; wait for the decisions of higher management; and shirk responsibility for implementation.

Chinese managers, and indeed workers, generally have a poor concept of quality management or quality control. Many foreign manufacturers complain that a great deal of their time and effort is taken up in constantly addressing issues of standard and consistency of product. This problem highlights the need for progressive implementation of Total Quality Management (TQM) programmes in Chinese industry from management down to the workplace.

However, their negative attitude towards participation does not mean that they do not have their own good ideas about quality improvement. Actually, most of them have a great deal of experience and knowledge in their particular field, and understand workplace issues very well. These middle managers can potentially become very active supporters of the joint venture, if a suitable corporate culture can be created which encourages participation in decision-making. To ensure this, provide a detailed job description to clarify each manager's rights and obligations, though it is impossible to cover every aspect of employment. It is important to create a corporate culture that contains some advantages of Western management and is, at the same time, acceptable to the Chinese staff. A harmonious and more democratic corporate culture can be best established through close contact between the two management teams from the very beginning. A period of intensive workplace training in your home organisation's operations room will go a long way towards convincing Chinese middle managers about the importance of substantial participation in joint venture decision-making and TQM policy implementation.

Managing Chinese Employees

First-line Chinese employees are an excellent group. They are deeply influenced by the traditional values of loyalty, kindness, collectivism and hierarchy. And in particular they have a strong sense of the virtue of repaying kindness or favours. They are completely loyal to higher management, and bear hardship in their total commitment to the goals and objectives of their enterprise, particularly if they feel their managers are able to take care of their special needs. Your management team must therefore first identify both the subjective and objective needs of workers, as well as those of lower and middle management, including the issues of workers' welfare and 'face protection'. Although you do not have to follow the welfare model of Chinese state-owned organisations, nevertheless to bring out the best in your employees it is necessary to design workplace packages that will ultimately create an open, consultative, progressive, cross-cultural and ultimately successful management culture.

These progressive management solutions can be a powerful weapon against a range of negative workplace values which can, if left unchecked, adversely affect enterprise effectiveness. For instance, most Chinese workers have little appreciation of competition and self-actualisation, as a result of the profound influence of hierarchical and collective values. In dealing with this, you must remember that you cannot expect too much from Chinese employees' without first investing time and energy in training. Chinese employees will avoid saying 'No' to their superiors about job-related issues, even though they may harbour some serious complaints about what they do and how it is done.

Again this is an issue of 'face', both of the individual employees and of their superiors.

In order to instil a culture of striving for organisational efficiency there are two final key points to remember.

The first is that training programmes, both in China, but especially overseas (if the cost is not prohibitive) are very valuable. So is a clear employee job description, which should solve most problems arising from employees who do not want to take responsibility for low work effectiveness. Linking a productivity-based incentive programme to individual achievement is another effective means of dramatically turning around employees' performance. Remember that some of these programmes are relatively new to China. While well established in the West, they will be seen as progressive and exciting innovations in China. These programmes will be especially effective if you can obtain the cooperation of the local Chinese Trade Union representatives, who can be used to negotiate an agreement which links productivity and positive cultural change to a range of workplace employees' welfare benefits.

The second point is that a dictatorial approach does not work well in China. Chinese employees expect to do what they are asked, but do not appreciate being shamed publicly by being ordered to perform, whether by foreign or Chinese joint venture managers. 'Face protection' makes most Chinese sensitive to direct criticism. You can overcome this by establishing a corporate culture from the very beginning of the joint venture that downplays hierarchical values and places a high premium on trust and common benefit.

Chapter Six

Chinese Government Officials

Coordinating Business Activities

In China the business world and government are closely connected. One of the vital aspects of doing business in China is dealing with officials. Most foreign businesspeople say that they feel uncomfortable having to work so closely with government at an operational level. They often complain about having to deal with what seems to be an army of bureaucrats when attempting to establish or promote their business. This situation arises because most Westerners do not understand the role of government in China's commercial life, nor do they appreciate that in China government systems permeate business at every level.

The first section of this chapter introduces the role of the Chinese Government in commerce. The second section examines ways of constructively working with officials of the Chinese bureaucracy. And the final section looks at the function of gift-giving in Chinese social life, and suggests ways of effectively establishing business relationships with government officials.

For most Westerners, their first reaction to official involvement in business is a state of culture shock. They are confused at being expected to show respect for officials without reservation. They object to having to give gifts to government functionaries, because they believe that it could be interpreted as 'corrupt' behaviour. However confusing or infuriating this may be, no matter how you feel about it, this is an unavoidable feature of business culture in China. It is reinforced by the ancient Chinese insistence on the importance of a 'seamless relationship between businesspeople and officialdom'. It is important to work with the system and not against it.

The Role of the Government in Commercial Activities

The close association between authority and economy almost completely characterises Chinese business culture. In recent years, as part of China's reform programme, the government has begun to reduce bureaucratic control in commerce wherever possible. However it will be a long time before this impacts on real business practice. To cope with official interference it is essential to first understand the economic role of the Chinese government and then identify strategies in order to enable your business to prosper by working closely with the Chinese bureaucracy.

Since the Open Door reforms of 1978, the Chinese Government has been working towards establishing a free market economic system with a Chinese flavour. One of the strongest elements of the emerging Chinese model is that the Communist Party and the Chinese Government still control many aspects of the economy. As a result, compared with Western developed countries, the role of the government in China's economy is powerful and pervasive. Besides functions common to most governments, China's various governmental organisations play an important role in the following five areas.

Involvement in Joint Venture Cooperation

The relevant Chinese government department is responsible for proposed cooperations between all foreign organisations and state-owned enterprises and some large collective-owned companies. This includes the establishment of joint ventures as well as foreign investment and trade exhibitions. Chinese companies must also secure permission to undertake overseas negotiations on behalf of their organisations.

On the surface it may appear that a foreign company is negotiating directly with an autonomous Chinese business partner. However, in reality discussions are actually held, although indirectly, with the controlling government department. Behind-the-scenes government officers supervise every state-owned or large collective-owned Chinese organisation.

Control of Market Price

Quite distinct from the practice of Western free market economies, governments at various levels in China have a special office called the Price Bureau. This department is responsible for generating market price policies and then monitoring their implementation. Although the prices of individual products or services can be determined by enterprises themselves, Chinese businesses or joint ventures must report their current price schedules to the Price Bureau for consideration. The Chinese central government argues that the market price of most goods and services must be measured and controlled in order to identify and avoid political disillusionment with economic reform. According to the government, 'public panic' over price must be avoided at all cost. 'Panic', they argue, could precipitate hyper-inflation and currency collapse. Because of this officials of the Price Bureau take their responsibilities very seriously. Among other activities, they annually audit the prices of commodities in the light of government price policies. Apart from the consumer prices of food, cigarettes, alcohol and so on, the Price Bureau regularly check costs associated with services such as tourism and transportation.

The Price Bureau has a statutory right to fine anyone whose product or service violates official price regulations. In addition to price, the type or variety of products or services offered by a foreign company or joint venture is also under the administrative jurisdiction of the Price Bureau. Contact with the Price Bureau is therefore unavoidable if you supply products or services to the Chinese market. In May 1998 the first Price Law in China will come into effect. This stipulates that the prices of commodities are to be adjusted by market supply and demand, but that the central government reserves the right, if necessary, to control prices, especially the prices of staple goods.

Financial Control

China's financial system is entirely controlled by the government. The banking and insurance industries and other peak financial institutions all are owned by the state. Top management in these industries are appointed and directly supervised by the government. Foreign investment enterprises may however apply for loans from the Bank of China or any other commercial Chinese or China-based bank as they would elsewhere. They can also take out business loans from any branch of a foreign bank located in China that has been issued with a banking licence by the government, or from China's banks located in Hong Kong or Macao. The Bank of China and other commercial banks must follow official policy regarding certain business conditions. Examples are:

- The enterprise must be registered with the Bureau of the Administration of Industry and Commerce before obtaining the appropriate operating licences.
- Following this the business must open an account with the Bank of China.
- The required register capital must be paid on time and legally confirmed.
- The relevant governmental planning department must approve the asset investment of the project or enterprise.

- The enterprise must provide evidence that they have the financial capacity to repay bank interest and capital in a specified period.

Direct Management of Large Enterprises

Some key industries, such as rail, aviation and telecommunications, are not open to foreign management or investment. These basic utilities are operated and controlled by the Chinese Government. In these state-owned enterprises the government has decreased administrative interference; however, the relationship between most state-owned enterprises and key governmental departments is still very close. The three utilities mentioned are all examples of state-owned enterprises controlled by the Chinese Government at central, provincial and municipal levels.

In all these enterprises the government usually appoints a general manager or Chairman of the board, though they may also be 'elected' by employees. For example, the provincial government appoints the general manager of an enterprise administered by the provincial government. In addition, there is normally a personnel department at every level of government, controlled by representatives of the Communist Party. In fact, Communist Party cadres are in charge of most enterprise personnel appointments. The Party sees personnel as under its jurisdiction, because the government sees the growth of business as essential to the national interest—currently approximately 50% of all China's revenue comes from state-owned enterprises, with 70% of employees in cities and towns involved.

Control of Foreign Investment

The Chinese Government has controlled the level and type of foreign investment since the very beginning of the Open Door policy. In May 1995 this control was formalised in the State Council Foreign Investment Leadership Team. It is now the role of the Deputy Prime Minister of the State Council to formally supervise the many government departments which administer all foreign investment. These include:

- The State Planning Commission

- The State Economic and Trade Commission
- The Special Zone Office of the State Council
- The Ministry of Foreign Trade and Economic Cooperation
- The Ministry of Personnel
- The Ministry of Finance
- The People's Bank of China
- The Bank of China
- The Ministry of Labour
- The State Tax Bureau
- The Administrative Bureau of Commerce and Trade
- The Bureau of Justice
- The Bureau of Commodity Inspection.

Each of those government departments is in charge of different aspects of foreign investment management. The three main areas of their responsibilities are:

- Checking and approving all foreign investment projects in China—details of this are provided in Chapter 5.
- Supervising the legal operating activities of foreign companies. The relevant government departments monitor whether these enterprises and companies implement their signed contracts properly; whether they inject the prescribed amount of capital into the project on time according to the terms of their contract; whether they run their business legally; and whether they protect and maintain their employees' rights and working conditions.
- Inspecting whether the enterprise provides the necessary services for the establishment and operation of their business. This involves these government departments taking responsibility for assisting with difficulties that occur in the everyday running of foreign investment projects.

The pervasive role of government in China's economy is reflected in a popular expression among Chinese businesspeople, which maintains, 'One can keep oneself preoccupied trying to solving a matter for three years, whereas an official in charge will solve the same problem in an instant'. This indicates that businesspeople in China believe that officials of the government are essential allies whose support ensures the smooth running of business.

There are many cases where local or provincial officials have come to the rescue of Chinese or foreign companies. Officials of different departments have the power to determine which investments have priority or how and where resources are distributed, and in recruiting or selecting and in promoting the best trained and most appropriate staff. Consequently, Chinese businesspeople and managers understand that without the cooperation of the appropriate officials, business approvals are unobtainable. They also appreciate that if they want to raise the profile of their business in the community or promote their goods or services across China, then they simply must look for ways of showing their respect to those officials who hold a position of authority or influence over their interests.

Clearly the role of the official in China is pre-eminent. It is not only based on practical economic and political power, but also on a number of other factors, social, cultural and administrative. These factors include:

- Chinese tradition advocates hierarchical values, which determine that respect for officials is automatic.
- Business success is typified by a striving for a 'seamless relationship between business and officialdom'. As we noted in Chapter 2, this means that Chinese businesspeople still believe that official power is a kind of guarantee for success in business.
- China's resources are constantly in a state of shortage. The central government is unable to satisfy all the demands made upon its financial, material or administrative resources. It is very hard to guarantee that these resources (which are controlled by officials) are channelled equitably. Some officials may take advantage of their positions to further their own interests, which makes a cooperative relationship with officials even more necessary.
- Some public officials abuse their powers, resulting in corruption. Currently the Chinese administrative system cannot effectively avoid this happening.

Finding the appropriate way to contact government officials is the practical concern of anyone wanting to do business in China. Identifying and appropriating the skills of contact with officialdom is the necessary first step towards building up acumen in this area, and is one of the keys to exploring new business opportunities in China.

Communicating Effectively with Government Officials

A Chinese proverb maintains that 'strangers should follow local customs'. As a visitor in China, you must learn about local life if you want to be accepted by a new community in a new place. The Open Door reforms have ensured that China has its own unique administrative and political system, a very durable one. Since you cannot change the system, in the spirit of the Chinese proverb, it is more prudent to learn how to play the game by Chinese rules.

Avoid Discussion about Political Issues

There is a popular expression in the Chinese business community that says, 'Focus solely on business in the commercial world'. This wise saying emphasises that businesspeople must follow the rules of commerce and concentrate on business itself. Chinese businesspeople are likewise fond of saying that 'Business is business, don't be interrupted by other matters or purposes and don't apply the rules of other fields to the business world'.

The Chinese central government, like governments everywhere, often creates links between commercial activities and political interests. However, officials at lower levels, especially those in charge of economic and trade affairs and the average Chinese businessperson, are very uncomfortable about making a connection between business and politics. They normally avoid any discussion about political reform, for instance, when engaging in business with foreigners, especially in the initial stage of contact. Chinese businesspeople are very concerned about following the rules of business, believing that sensitive political comments can easily be misunderstood, and that political discussions may be detrimental to their professional prospects. One of the reasons for this discomfort is that government officials are always on the alert for anyone, including foreign businesspeople, who continuously raise political issues during business discussions, even though this may be a matter of personal curiosity and not intended to cause offence. Since the motives of such a person are automatically under suspicion, officials in charge of business are very cautious about dealing with them. They are watched very closely. Indeed, officials may decide to discontinue negotiations on the grounds that their motives are doubtful. We advise you strongly not to publicly or indiscreetly raise political topics with your Chinese counterparts, as you run the risk of causing embarrassment and a 'loss of face' for both parties.

Respecting Officials' Authority

Because China is a society that has a strong historical and contemporary sense of hierarchy, Chinese government officials have a deeply rooted understanding of the power of authority compared to their Western counterparts. In China, officials and bureaucrats link respect for authority with respect for their position of authority. At times some officials are actually too sensitive about their authority, and this arouses unnecessary enmity in the hearts of people who have to deal with them. If you wish to navigate beyond officialdom, you must learn to conceal your dislike for these overbearing and oversensitive officials. It is in fact advisable that you show unqualified respect for Chinese officials wherever possible by arranging a variety of special activities in their honour. We advise you further to make a courtesy telephone call to the official in charge of the department dealing with your project on your first visit to China. After this a dinner or banquet can be arranged so that the two of you can meet and initiate face-to-face negotiations.

Another good idea is to invite the appropriate officials to visit the project office or plant on a regular basis. This creates goodwill, particularly while you are waiting for project approval or licensing. The purpose of these activities are to deliver an unambiguous message that you are fully aware of the official's position, authority and power, and that you recognise and acknowledge that the official's support is crucial for the project's success.

Referring to Chinese officials in the correct way is another aspect of showing respect for official authority. Quite different from the West, Chinese people are not accustomed to calling each other by their first names, except to show that an intimate friendship relationship already exists. On most occasions, especially where any kind of social hierarchical relationship is involved, Chinese people call each other by their surname followed by their position title. For example, school students in China cannot call their teacher by their first name or even by their title, such as 'Mr Wang' or 'Mrs Lu'; they must call their teacher by their surname followed by 'teacher'. This custom is strongly reflected in the social intercourse of Chinese officials and others. Chinese officials definitely expect others to call them by their position title, such as 'Li Mayor', 'Zhang Secretary' or 'Liu Director'. This does not mean that you will be rejected by Chinese officialdom if you inadvertently call an official by their first name, or if you use 'Mr' or 'Mrs', but it does reflect very favourably if you refer to them in the correct way, so that they immediately feel that they are respected.

Friendship Contact through a Personal Channel

'Connections' or *guanxi* are very important in Chinese society, even though nowadays technological or academic qualifications are almost of equal high standing. It is well known that in China 'who you know' is more important than 'what you know'. *Guanxi* is the greatest advantage to a career in business. As we described in Chapter 3, personal relationships based on feelings and trust are essential psychological components to achieving a successful business outcome. You can easily develop your business if you enjoy close ties of friendship with the right powerful official. The best way of establishing this important relationship is to make contact through a personal channel.

Normally, it would not be acceptable in the West for officials or businesspeople to discuss business after business hours, whether formally or informally. On most occasions, Western businesspeople prefer not to be disturbed during what they believe is the time set aside for their private lives. Consequently, Western officials or businesspeople rarely print their home telephone numbers on their business cards, reserving this privileged information for those who have a formal working relationship with them. This however is not always the case in China. Many Chinese officials (except very senior officers of state) and businesspeople not only print their name, position, title, telephone and fax numbers of their working place, but also put their home telephone number and residential address on the same card, indicating that anyone can contact them after business hours if necessary.

The Chinese make little distinction between private and public life. They often work many hours beyond work time, especially if they believe that it is necessary. For some businesspeople, schedules in their non-business hours are much more hectic than during business hours. People in the Chinese commercial community even presume that a person's business will decline if they have nothing to do, or no one to deal with, after working hours. This can be seen in the following illustration.

In 1994 a Chinese businesswoman tried to introduce a foreign company to a Chinese counterpart with a view to working together on a China-based project. She accompanied the managing director of the foreign company to Beijing for further business discussions after extensive long-distance negotiations. Like other Chinese businesspeople, the general manager of the Chinese company treated the foreign guest generously during his trip to China. However, the foreign managing director found that the Chinese general manager talked almost continuously on his mobile phone—when he picked them up from the airport, at the hotel and during dinner in the evening. The foreign managing director asked the Chinese businesswoman, 'Why couldn't the Chinese general manager finish his work within work hours?' and then commented that 'the Chinese manager must not be an efficient manager'. Although the reason for the behaviour was explained at length, the foreign director was still confused, and made it very clear that he did not appreciate this Chinese manager's behaviour. Ironically, while the Chinese manager was undoubtedly busy, his behaviour may have been partly intended to impress on his Western counterpart how important, essential, hardworking, diligent and above all efficient he really was. Clearly, there exists a marked difference between the two managers' perspectives of what constitutes efficiency.

According to Chinese business culture, if something cannot be discussed with an official or bureaucrat in the workplace or at a formal meeting, and an opportunity arises to talk to them in their home or during an informal occasion, then the Chinese manager must seize the moment. According to the Chinese, this is truly an efficient use of their valuable time.

What is difficult for many Westerners to appreciate is that business discussed in the home or at an informal occasion is sometimes treated with more seriousness than business raised in an official forum. For this reason it is preferable to spend a substantial amount of time becoming familiar with Chinese officials. You have to be prepared to put aside concepts such as 'work time' and 'leisure time'; they are to all intents and purposes interchangeable in China. You need to discover a particular official's likes and dislikes, ambitions and special talents if you are to successfully to mesh business and recreation. Appreciating this vital inside information is the most effective way of establishing a friendship relationship with Chinese government officials, because ultimately these relationships will make the difference between business success and failure.

Treating Chinese Officials as a Network

Currently, the Chinese management system is characterised by a great deal of bureaucratic overlap. To get something done, a businessperson has to deal with a number of different departments and with a number of different bureaucrats or managers. This is illustrated by the fact that many Chinese companies often have many deputy directors for each senior managerial position. Deputy directors are supposed to be responsible for different aspects of operations, although from an effective management point of view the nature and amount of their work does not often appear to necessitate more than one position.

Each deputy director has the authority to participate in the decision-making process and to give an opinion on final decisions. Unfortunately, these deputies may have different opinions. This type of organisational structure obviously results in inefficient management practice. It also causes a great deal of confusion for anyone who is trying to do business with a particular enterprise or company. This is especially vexing when one manager objects to the final decision and the others do not. Under these circumstances the project will have to be reconsidered. This same situation is mirrored in government departments because they have the same overlapping organisation structures.

The same types of problems can also arise between organisations. Sometimes an important project or proposal needs to be approved by a number of government departments simultaneously. For example, a state-owned enterprise may be a subsidiary organisation of the Ministry of Telecommunications while also under the supervision of the provincial government. In this case, both governments have the final say on management decisions. This situation is further complicated by the fact that within departments there can exist inter-departmental factional divergences.

Directly contacting and building up relationships with all relevant officials or managers is the best way to operate smoothly in China. This is especially important when dealing with large enterprises or companies. Whatever levels of government or management problems occur, you must coordinate these complex relationships by treating officialdom as a network. That is, you must identify everyone who impacts on the project, and single out those most responsible for making the final decision for 'special face' or special respect and attention. Then you must contact them in the proper way.

You can never presume that talking with one official in charge of a particular affair can settle your business. An official may promise to support your business, but later may tell you that they can no longer help with your case. One of the reasons for this refusal might be because the official's colleagues, especially their manager, were not consulted in the correct hierarchical manner, or perhaps were not convinced of the appropriate manner of approaching the problem at hand. As usual, the best way to overcome this problem, and most other problems in Chinese business, is to invest time and effort in accurately identifying the top official, building up a personal relationship with the key decision-makers, and arguing your case in a spirit of friendship, respect and cooperation.

Here is an example of why the relevant Chinese officials must be treated as a network.

A foreign company intended to invest in a project in one of China's counties. On the surface there appeared to be no problems associated with the project, especially after representatives of the Chinese company took the opportunity to demonstrate great hospitality towards the foreign delegation. The problem was, however, that the foreign company incorrectly presumed that the head of the county was the only person they needed to communicate with. The project had no sooner started than it ran into serious trouble when the local secretary of the Communist Party Committee raised an objection. The secretary felt that the company had ignored him, as he had not been introduced to the delegation or briefed about their operational goals.

What the foreign delegation quickly learned was that, according to China's current bureaucratic system, the authority of a local Communist Party secretary is higher than the administrative head of the county. This company would not have had met any resistance from local officials if their representatives had properly contacted *both* the secretary of the CCP committee and the administrative head of the county.

The Role of Gift-giving in Business

Gift-giving in Chinese Social Life

Gift-giving is one of the salient characteristics of Chinese culture. It is used widely by most Chinese people to fulfil a variety of social obligations. Its role in Chinese society is similar to that of the banquet in business culture, but it is more popular than that, as it is easily and inexpensively arranged (although in China gifts can also be very expensive). This custom profoundly influences Chinese social life, sometimes to an unbalanced extent unacceptable to both Westerners and Chinese. For instance, sometimes Chinese factory workers may have to borrow money to buy gifts for a variety of reasons. There may be so many events that require the giving of gifts that these workers cannot afford to meet all their obligations from their salary alone: a colleagues' wedding, a graduation, a child's birthday, the celebration associated with moving into a new house and so on. It is also said that some overseas Chinese originally from Mainland China are worried about returning to their homeland because they feel they cannot afford to buy enough valuable or appropriate gifts to satisfy their relatives and friends. This custom is also a particular feature of Chinese customer psychology. The impact of gift-giving on consumer behaviour is discussed in Chapters 7 and 8.

Occasionally gifts serve as a token for monetary remuneration, with or without the receiver's agreement. However, on most occasions gifts are more important as symbols of respect and esteem. When they send someone a precious gift, many Chinese like to say 'A thrifty gift cannot show my great esteem for you'.

In China gift-giving is related to 'face protection' and hierarchy. Appropriately the type and value of a gift should reflect the gift receiver's status, rank and taste. A low-quality, tasteless or inappropriate gift will embarrass both the giver and receiver. Generally speaking, both the status and income of the giver must match the value and quality of the gift. Higher-ranking people receive correspondingly more expensive presents than lower-ranking people, if the receiver is in a group at the same hierarchical level. If a giver has a high income, then they must give a gift of relative high value, otherwise they will be thought to be stingy or miserly. If they have have a low income, but send a valuable or thoughtful gift, then the receiver will think that the giver is generous and take their friendship seriously. In this case, both the 'faces' of the giver and receiver have been protected. Expensive liquor, wine, cigarettes and valuable works of art or craft are the most usual gifts presented or exchanged between Chinese people.

Establishing a Relationship with Chinese Officials

Every section of Chinese social, political and economic life is obsessed with the traditional custom of gift-giving. Sending gifts to officials is likewise a Chinese phenomenon. A common Chinese expression maintains that 'an official never blames a gift-giver'. Commercial activities are regarded as a forum for establishing friendship relationships between people, and gift-giving plays a pre-eminent role in this procedure. Officials, like everyone else, like to receive gifts, including appropriate gifts from businesspeople. In Chinese business culture, sending gifts to officials has a number of specific functions, such as catching an official's attention, building up goodwill, exploring the possibility of establishing a personal relationship for the purpose of long-term cooperation, obtaining the official's support, and hoping for reciprocation in the form of issuing an operating licence or approving a business application in a legal but timely fashion.

Generally, there are two ways of sending gifts to officials. One is to send the gift to the official individually; the other is to send the gift to the appropriate department marked especially for the attention of a particular official or officials. The former is often executed in a private manner in order to obtain individual support. The latter is a public display of respect that 'gives face' and therefore strengthens cooporation between two organisations. For instance, during festival time a subsidiary organisation may send their products or other goods as gifts to the department that supervises it.

We strongly encourage you to familiarise yourself with the wisdom of this custom. If correctly applied, it can make the difference between success and failure in the Chinese market. If you do not apply it appropriately, a Chinese business partner will conclude that you are not a person they can easily have dealings with.

Based on each specific situation, it is important to answer three questions before deciding to send a gift: One, should a gift be sent to a particular official? Two, what gift should be sent? Finally, how should the gift be sent?

However, before we discuss these questions, it is necessary to point out that not every Chinese official expects a gift in the course of normal business. Many senior officials may refuse it as a matter of integrity. Sending a gift to this type of official may be detrimental to the giver's business or may result in an embarrassing 'loss of face'. On the other hand, a businessperson would not receive any support from an official who appreciates gifts if the gift were sent in an inappropriate manner. Some gifts must be presented in public and some in secret. Overseas-produced, high-quality, unique and thoughtful goods or works of art make the most impressive gifts.

In Western countries, someone who receives a gift normally opens the gift in front of the giver and others so they can demonstrate their appreciation for the giver's generosity. In contrast, Chinese people do not open gifts in front of the giver, believing it impolite. They think that this action indicates that they are either greedy or want to evaluate the gift publicly and therefore risk offending both the giver and the receiver. For the same reason, a Chinese official will occasionally appear unwilling to accept a gift. Generally this is a display of either caution or courtesy, and the giver is expected to persist with the offer.

Gift-giving and Anti-corruption Skills

A few powerful Chinese officials make use of the gift-giving custom to solicit bribes. Under Chinese law, an employee who takes advantage of their authority within the government system by accepting a bribe commits a crime, and both the briber and the receiver can be prosecuted. The most difficult question to answer is, how do you differentiate between a gift and a bribe? Unfortunately, or rather fortunately (for some people), Chinese law does not distinguish gifts from bribes in terms of value or a particular standard. The difference is very subtle and involves both cultural and economic issues, and may depend on the receiver's means of obtaining the item and the way in which the gift is conveyed. However, we strongly advise you not to dispense with gift-giving simply because of this ambiguity, especially if you want to be successful in China. In most circumstances this action is an entirely accepted custom. It is one of the keys to open the door to business success, or as an oil to lubricate the bureaucratic machine. No one wants to get themselves into hot water by being identified as corrupt. The issue, then, is how to differentiate between acceptable and unacceptable gift-giving.

At present, corruption in China is a serious problem. The centralised control of commercial activities, the underdeveloped Chinese legal system and the influence of 'a seamless relationship between business and officialdom' have combined to encourage corrupt behaviour at almost every level. Ordinary Chinese, including businesspeople, hate the corrupt behaviour of some governmental officials, especially those who abuse their power for personal gain to the detriment of honest business and national development. Most Chinese people support the central government in their attempts to stamp out corruption. However, like everywhere there is always a gap between hope and reality. There still exist many officials who ask for bribes both directly and indirectly. Usually, local officials who have the power to deal directly with foreign or local businesses have more opportunity to commit corrupt acts. For example, an electricity connection for an office or manufacturing plant may be delayed by an unreasonable period of time. One of the possible reasons for this may be that the official in charge of granting a connection is indirectly asking for a bribe—the delay may indicate that his or her 'requirement' has not been satisfied.

To protect your business interests, you need to learn the skills of denying or avoiding bribery. This is a difficult learning process. Clearly you must handle the issue strategically so as to gain official help in business without having to resort to corrupt practices yourself.

First, show respect for an official in charge by sending an appropriate gift or gifts. At the same time, you could make it known that you have a personal relationship with the most senior Chinese officials (if indeed you have). Because of the hierarchical nature of Chinese society, this will send an unambiguous message to lower level officials that they should avoid asking for bribes. Sometimes a foreign counterpart can hire a Chinese associate who is a lawyer, legal consultant or law enforcement officer with a reputation for honesty, and arrange for them to be introduced to Chinese officials during negotiations. In addition, you could invite these same officials to join the negotiating team at the banquet table.

The second way to deal with corruption is to tell the official that their 'personal requirement' is hard to meet. You should then suggest that you are obliged to report this 'new information' back to the headquarters of the company before a final decision can be made. Make a special point of emphasising that your company follows high ethical standards which specifically prohibit under-the-table payments, and that you are bound by those standards. Do not exhibit anger or strong emotion. If the Chinese official persists in indicating that a larger contribution is required in order to achieve a bureaucratic objective, apologise sincerely, and stress that if you were to agree to any kind of unauthorised payment then you would be dismissed from your organisation.

Thirdly, if the official openly and continuously insists on the payment of a bribe, say that under the circumstances you must inform them that you are to meet with their superior for further discussions or that you are obliged, or indeed have been requested, to report all problems with your business in China to the relevant department. If the corrupt individual continues to be uncooperative, it may help to discuss your problem in private with someone higher up in the chain of command. If the higher official agrees to grant the request, the subordinate must act. Never use this strategy as an open threat, since in China a humiliated official may do their best to frustrate your every effort.

Chapter Seven

Chinese Consumer Psychology

The Characteristics of the Chinese Market

Currently China's average per capita yearly income is around US$655 (1997). According to this index, China ranks economically in the middle of the world's less-developed countries. However, it is impossible to calculate the purchasing power of China's various consumer groups by using average income as the sole guide. The Chinese market is very illusory. It is a market where the wealthy may 'spend gold on one throw'—for instance where a businessperson may pay

US$1000 dollars for one restaurant meal, while most ordinary people maintain the convention of thrift and count every cent towards a purchase.

As a result of the late Deng Xiao Ping's policy of 'a portion of the population must become rich first', income disparity between social classes in Chinese society has become marked. In China's move towards a market economy with a Chinese flavour, levels of income have become relatively unpredictable. The rapid rise of certain income groups has produced a wealth gap, which has had a profound impact on the Chinese market and on consumer psychology.

The Psychology of Chinese Consumers

There are six outstanding dimensions to Chinese consumer psychology, resulting from the peculiarities of Chinese culture and certain government policies.

Saving Prior to Consuming

Chinese customers insist that consumption must be based on previous or past savings. Chinese people avoid spending money on medium or large purchases without first having planned and then saved. In contrast, consumer behaviour in many Western countries indicates that consumption is based on present and future income. For example, a Chinese person will typically purchase furnishings worth US$2000 by paying cash following a long period of saving, while a Westerner will typically pay for their high price items by instalment or by credit. Significantly, the cost of the goods may constitute six months' wages for a Chinese factory worker, but only two weeks for a Westerner working in the same employment classification.

It comes as no surprise then that the rate of personal savings in China is high compared with many other countries. According to a People's Bank of China report, in 1997 the combined savings of China's urban dwellers was US$532.893 billion. A survey conducted in China's five largest cities (Beijing, Chongqing, Guengzhou, Shenyang and Shanghai) revealed that 48% of families held average savings of over 10 000 *RMB yuan* (about $US1209), and that 15.4% of families in these cities held shares or bonds worth in excess of 4000 *RMB yuan* (about $US483). (Chinese currency is explained in the Almanac at the end of this book.)

Chinese consumers are not accustomed to applying for credit to buy relatively inexpensive goods. One of the reasons for this is that China's banks did not offer loans for the purchase of any private-purpose durable commodity until the early 1990s. Even now, because of the continued banking restrictions in China, most ordinary salary earners are not eligible for bank loans anyway. While a small number of Chinese consumers will only apply for a loan to buy a car or a house, they will seldom ever consider the possibility of applying for credit to purchase small items such a refrigerator, television set, furniture or overseas travel. If someone borrows money to buy a television set, for instance, their friends and relatives will consider them both foolish and a poor manager of their personal finances.

The Chinese attitudes towards the 'avoidance of uncertainty' and 'face protection' are two of the reasons for this particular feature of Chinese consumer psychology. Many Chinese people believe that borrowing money to buy goods is a form of public embarrassment. It causes them to 'lose face' with their contemporaries, because Chinese people are group-oriented and like to maintain a close relationship within their respective communities. Public and private life have no clear distinction drawn between the two: people within a particular community or network involve themselves in most aspects of each others' daily lives.

For most Chinese consumers the act of purchasing is not just a simple transaction: it demonstrates an individual's financial capacity and social status. This in turn serves to meet the individual's psychological need for social esteem. In this way the community views an application to borrow money in two ways: one, that the applicant did not have sufficient earning capacity to purchase the goods in the first place; or alternativeely, that the person did not have the patience or self-control to save.

Finally, borrowing money from others in China has traditionally been seen as a risky activity. Most ordinary Chinese would feel more comfortable in waiting a little longer and saving a little harder so that they would be able to pay cash for their purchases. These cultural values, together with the realities of the present banking system in China, all reinforce the habit of saving prior to consuming. This profoundly influences the buying behaviour of the majority of Chinese consumers.

'Vying for Purchasing'

The other outstanding psychological characteristic of Chinese consumer behaviour is that of 'vying with others for the glory of purchasing'. The buying behaviour of most Chinese people is strongly influenced by a number of reference groups, which generate a strong desire to buy relatively expensive items, especially when a particular item has become popular or has already been bought by relatives, friends or neighbours. Some people who cannot afford to buy a popular product immediately may be driven half mad by the 'vying' psychology and will concentrate all their efforts on saving. They will even reduce spending on the necessities of daily life for a short period in order to save for this particular purpose. And because of the closeness of group members within the Chinese community, the popularity of a given product may increase rapidly. Furthermore, Chinese consumers are more likely to accept a product if product information is spread through both informal and personal channels as well as formal or official channels of communication.

A traditional value, also connected with the 'vying for purchasing' mentality, is the Chinese value of 'absolute egalitarianism'. This not only influences people's views about wealth allocation, but has an impact on their buying behaviour as well. Most ordinary people in China believe that there should not be a wealth or standard of living gap between people within the same social class. They would feel 'a loss of face' if they could not buy an expensive item, particularly an item which was already currently available to others within the same social class.

As a result, 'vying for purchasing' is a prominent feature of Chinese consumer psychology. Often Chinese customers will rush to purchase the same kinds of goods and services in a particular field in a particular period. The habit of saving before consuming provides the financial and psychological basis for 'vying for purchasing'. Ordinary people always have money put away for such 'necessities'. For instance, every brand of home air conditioner in the Beijing market sold out in the summer of 1997. Although this was a particularly hot summer, sales were mostly attributable to the fact that air-conditioning units became the sort of fashionable commodity which Beijing consumers were most 'vying to buy'.

Influence of the One-Child Policy on Family Purchases

The child's role in family purchasing behaviour is now well recognised by marketing theorists around the world. Children are especially influential in how their parents make decisions about food, toys, clothing, vacations, recreation and automobiles. This characteristic is fully evident in the Chinese market. It is particularly relevant given the powerful influence of China's policy of one child per family. In China, family purchases (at least in urban areas)—except for the purchase of expensive goods or very basic necessities—are dominated by the single child's needs and desires.

The Chinese Government's population control programme stipulates that families are only allowed to have one child. Currently, this policy is not well implemented in rural areas. However, due to the insistence of the government, and for economic reasons, this policy has been accepted by almost all young urban-dwelling couples, especially in the large cities of Beijing, Shanghai and Guangzhou and so on. Traditional Chinese culture and the extended family structure (consisting of many related adults and one child) has resulted in the child becoming the most privileged consumer in Chinese society.

The relationship between generations within a Chinese family is very close. The concept of 'family' differs from that in some Western countries, where it tends to be more nuclear. In China, the younger generation has a moral obligation to care for the elderly, especially when the latter becomes dependent because of old age or infirmity. In turn, parents have a moral and social obligation to care for their child for most of their lives. A very old Chinese saying maintains that 'if a son has not been properly educated or cultivated, then it is not his fault but the fault of his father'. Parents everywhere, regardless of country or culture, are responsible for their children's material welfare and education. Beyond this, cultural differences emerge. Children in the West are expected to be independent after they reach the age of 18 years. But in China, parents are expected to continue to support their children in most aspects of living and development long after they come of age. Most Chinese parents dedicate their entire lives to supporting every aspect of their child's growth and development. Most Western parents are grateful for the day their children leave the nest and become independent adults.

The structure of the Chinese one-child family reinforces this sense of parental obligation—the child is the focus of both the immediate and the extended family. Because of this, Chinese parents are willing to suffer any hardship in order to make their child's life a successful and comfortable one. They do their utmost to provide their child with the best education, the finest food, and the most modern clothes. For example, the price of Beijing-produced milk is three times less expensive than the milk imported from Australia or Holland, but the quality of imported milk is much higher than that of the local product. Many parents in Beijing buy Australian or Dutch products for their child, but drink nothing but the local product themselves, or go without altogether for the sake of their children. Market research has indicted that Australian and Dutch milk products sell very well in the Beijing market because they 'are the best', and Chinese parents want nothing but the best for their 'golden child'.

Many young Chinese parents save for years after they first marry to buy a piano or other expensive musical instrument for their child. Tuition can then begin before the child starts school. Early and intensive tuition is believed to give children a head start in the highly competitive Chinese school system. This involves costly training classes that require disciplined saving on the part of parents. Expensive but thorough training for

China's present generation of urban 'golden children' is also available for instruction in the English language, computer studies, drawing, music, mathematics and Mandarin calligraphy. Chinese parents are willing to spend a great deal of money on their child, as they believe education guarantees a prosperous and happy life. Providing these educational programmes becomes the almost compulsory responsibility of all parents.

In China most people know nothing about Mother's or Father's Day. However, everyone knows that 1 June is International Child's Day. Parents, grandparents, friends, and school communities all celebrate this important day by holding elaborate ceremonies and by lavishing gifts on their children. In addition, during other important occasions, such as the traditional Chinese spring festival, the child often receives a generous allotment of pocket money from relatives or the friends of their parents. In the first instance this is because the giving of gifts is part of traditional Chinese festival culture, but it is also because the 'golden child' has become the focus of the entire family.

As a result, children's consumer goods, ranging from exotic and nutritional foods to 'study aids' (which are supposed to develop intelligence), all sell extremely well in the Chinese market. Child consumers have already become one of the most profitable targets of Chinese business.

The Influence of Social Relationships on Consumer Psychology

Just as interpersonal relationships play a crucial role in Chinese social life, so does Chinese consumer psychology. Accordingly, in the Chinese market, there are many occasions that require gift-giving purchases. Many Chinese consumers buy luxury goods not for personal consumption, but as gifts. While gift-giving has been covered at length in Chapter 6, it bears reinforcing in the light of consumer behaviour.

The purpose of gift-giving is to strengthen a wide range of relevant or mutually beneficial interpersonal relationships. For example, a valuable gift is often presented to a boss before or after an employee receives a pay rise or promotion, or as an expression of a close and successful personal or business friendship. A special token of appreciation may be presented to the principal of a good school for processing a child's enrolment. A gift may be lovingly presented to the aged in order to demonstrate filial piety; to a teacher for his or her special help with a child's study; to a doctor for providing immediate and expert treatment; or to a director of a housing committee for obtaining an accommodation allocation. In this the giver must select the right gift for the right person and occasion. The receiver's gender, likes and needs, social status and relative personal and professional value must be taken into account. The right time can be any time during a variety of special occasions, festivals or public holidays, all seen as good opportunities for establishing or strengthening relationships. In giving festive gifts, imported wines, flowers, expensive European wristwatches or exotic imported handicrafts are popular options, as are clothes, nutritional or novelty foods and fine linen, as well as electronic items such as television sets. However, what is as important as the gift itself is the way in which the gift is presented.

In terms of the needs and motives of gift-giving, Chinese consumers pay a great deal of attention to packaging. This is especially true of the giver's buying psychology. Because Chinese consumers are preoccupied with 'face', a person will select a particular item according to the method of presentation as much as for the type or quality. Since a gift is never opened in public, or in front of the receiver, the packaging must perfectly reflect the value of what is inside. The gift-wrapping must appear attractive and impressive. It must leave no doubt whatsoever in the mind of anyone that the giver highly esteems the receiver.

'Flaunting' Consumption

'Flaunting' consumer purchasing is intended to publicly demonstrate a consumer's wealth or status. In China this kind of behaviour is limited to a small but influential group within society, mainly composed of wealthy businesspeople, or state- and collective-owned enterprise managers who have access to expense accounts. For senior managers it is easy to spend organisational funds which are not theirs. Although these consumers are small in number, their purchasing power is huge.

Since the reforms of 1978, many Chinese businessmen and women have become millionaires. Many of these people have had no formal education. Some have humble backgrounds, having risen from the lower social stratum of Chinese society. Present-day Chinese society combines the traditional values of hierarchy and the modern one of respecting intelligence. There is little true respect for wealthy upstarts with little intellectual or cultural sophistication. In spite of possessing a great deal of money, the status of some of China's wealthy class is still quite low. These wealthy people often attempt to use their money to buy a reputation. In other words, they will try almost anything to achieve social esteem or 'face', including spending money on 'flaunting' purchases that the average Chinese consumer could never afford.

One day in 1990, a resident who appeared to be a simple peasant walked into a five-star hotel located in downtown Beijing, and enquired about accommodation. The receptionist informed the man that this particular hotel was not an appropriate place for him to stay. The receptionist's condescending manner enraged the peasant, who felt an acute 'loss of face'. He continually asked her about the cost of the room. The receptionist replied, 'Why do you ask this question, as clearly you can not afford even a fraction of the nightly tariff'. This time the man lost his temper completely, because there were many people in the hotel lobby watching the spectacle. The man retorted, 'I will stay in no place other than in the best room in this hotel'. 'The best room costs US$1200 a night', the receptionist answered. The man sarcastically replied, 'Only US$1200. I would pay US$2200 if necessary.' Finally this man of very humble appearance paid the appropriate tariff to stay in the hotels' VIP suite, though he needed a great deal of assistance in completing his registration form.

> Regardless of the receptionist's poor attitude towards the customer, the man's response was typical 'flaunting' behaviour of many of China's new rich.

Nightclubs in China's large cities are the main public forums for this type of 'flaunting'. In these places guests sit together to talk and drink a great deal of expensive imported spirits. Often brands will be valued at over US$200 a bottle—the more expensive and exclusive the brand, the more important it is to be seen drinking it. If one patron has paid US$50 to one of the nightclub entertainers to sing a particular song, another may offer US$100 for the same singer to sing the same song. The tune will then be performed, and dedicated to the highest bidder. The expenses of any one of these customers will often exceed several months' salary of an ordinary employee. Although the average Chinese consumer condemns this behaviour and the Chinese government strongly discourages 'non-thrifty conduct', 'flaunting' consumer behaviour can be seen everywhere in China. As a result of this phenomenon, services industries are booming, as are sales of imported luxury alcoholic drinks.

The Characteristics of Chinese Consumer Behaviour

China is a rapidly industrialising society that now produces a great deal of the world's capital goods and durable products. As China's economy continues to grow and change, incomes have increased rapidly. With this new-found wealth has come an insatiable appetite for luxurious goods and services.

Brand Loyalty versus Fashion Followers

Research into Chinese consumers in the 1980s concluded that most Chinese are brand loyal. While at the time this confirmed a long-held traditional Chinese value, the research is now partially out of date. Brand loyalty remains predominantly a characteristic of the older generation of Chinese consumers; nowadays, young Chinese hold no such sentiments at all.

In China, people aged over 55 years are unlikely to switch to other brands or products. They are more likely to believe that it is not worth the risk to abandon brand names that they have enjoyed for a long time. For them, trying new brands invites the possibility of a wrong purchase decision. The traditional values of 'a high avoidance of uncertainty' and 'maintaining a thrifty lifestyle' continue to impact strongly on them. Their tendency to plan ahead for large purchases dictates that they prefer less expensive familiar brands to higher priced new brands. The money saved on small, trusted items is put aside for larger, more expensive purchases. Older Chinese consumers make a purchase decision for expensive items relatively slowly and prudently.

Compared with the older generation, many younger upwardly mobile consumers are much more open-minded about new brands, new products and new ideas. It is this group that now has the stronger purchasing power. China's post-Open Door generation wants to accept anything new as long as it symbolises fashion, high social class or outstanding quality. Their penchant for reasonably highly priced brands or products is well known. Clearly the younger generation in China has been influenced by Western or modern tastes. American cigarettes, German cars, Japanese electronic products, French cosmetics, British beer and Australian milk all are in fashion and in favour. For China's new young rich, these products mean credibility. They are symbols of fashion, good taste and wealth. Flaunting these symbols tells the world that a particular consumer group is astute enough to recognise a trend, and then follow it. In China, trends come at a price. Imported products are expensive when compared to incomes. However, young Chinese consumers are willing to pay for fashionable items, especially if they are purchased as gifts, particularly in the case of teenagers and young women. Teenagers, as the product of the 'one-child' policy, have many opportunities to ask their parents to buy them well-known brands of footwear or clothing, even though these goods are usually many times more expensive than the local product.

Thanks to a broader range of choices, and 'vying for purchasing' psychology, many Chinese women are very concerned about keeping abreast of what clothes are fashionable; which cosmetics are being used by the rich and famous; and what new body-care services are coming on to the market. Unmarried women will not hesitate to spend most of their income on these goods and services. They make quick purchase decisions for expensive items and they pay for them in cash. For most Chinese women, in particular the younger generation, shopping in large department stores is one of the most pleasurable experiences in their lives. They browse stores, hunting for desirable products. Because of a general rise in the affluence of the entire country, consumers like to go shopping and select from a wide range of products. Many stores have responded to this new demand by staying open until 9pm every night.

Extravagant Spending versus Strict Budgeting

The general level of consumption in any modern economy is based on income levels. The growth of purchasing power is an indication that in China the average income has increased, and with it the quality of life for many people. Chinese retailers have responded by making a wide range of new goods available to all income levels.

Currently, most incomes in China arise from three sources. The first is from formal salaries and subsidies. Salaries are standardised nationally, according to each specific industry. A particular employee's additional subsidies or fringe benefits are dependant on specific organisational policy and their need, such as housing. In China, a poorly performing enterprise may not be able to issue any subsidies to its employees, while a profitable organisation may issue a subsidy higher than the actual set salary.

The second source of remuneration is referred to as 'grey income'—wages derived from informal or concurrent work. For example, manufacturing workers run street stalls to boost their incomes, or take night jobs after normal working hours. This group also includes university lecturers who provide consultancy or training programmes to business, and enterprise managers who may hold conjoint appointments with different organisations.

The third source is 'black income', resulting from illegal, corrupt or immoral activities. Examples are a government official who obtains a 'back-hander' or a commission for speeding up the bureaucratic process, or a doctor who receives an extra payment for the offer of better treatment. Clearly the line between acceptable and corrupt behaviour can be fine, at least to Western eyes. As in any society, intention is fundamental to determing what is 'black' and what 'white'.

Senior managers working in foreign companies and joint ventures, owners of private enterprises, contractors of projects, popular actors and actresses, as well as doctors earn a great deal more than the average Chinese employee. A survey in China's *Labour Daily*, April 1995, reported that the average monthly salary of Chinese employees in 20 foreign-owned companies was 3620 *RMB yuan* (about US$437), much higher than the average wage paid by Chinese organisations. The survey indicated that department managers' monthly salary in the same 20 foreign organisations was 7369 *RMB yuan* (about US$889), with a deputy managing director on 9978 *RMB yuan* (about US$1204) a month. The Chinese magazine *Reform* (No. 2, 1995) reported that there were over 2 million millionaires in China. Hence, in China there are people who only earn 300 *RMB yuan* a month (about $US36), while others can earn 20 000 *RMB yuan* a month (about $US2418). Because of this income disparity, many people, including China's millionaire families, can afford to buy anything they like, while others have to budget diligently for each and every major purchase. Since the Chinese population consists predominantly of the latter, who carefully consider whether the price and quality of a product is reasonable before making a purchase, a very wide range of goods can be sold successfully in the Chinese market. Notwithstanding this, the most famous and exclusive imported brands in the world have loyal customers in China, as do some low-priced, reasonable quality imported goods.

Purchases: Shrewd and Attentive or Bold and Generous

China is a large country, and consumer culture varies across different regions. The country can be roughly divided into two large regions: south China and north China, divided by the Yangtze River. There are obvious differences in consumer culture between the north and the south.

Generally speaking, the consumers of south China are more careful about calculating the value of their purchases. They are also more likely to budget for goods than are the consumers of north China. They are more likely to carefully compare the price and quality of goods and services before making a purchase decision. Southern Chinese understand and follow fashion, and generally select goods that are suitable for their social class or profession.

In contrast, the consumers of north China spend money more freely and generously. The average income of people in the north of China is less than that of southerners, primarily due to an imbalance in the development of regional economies. However, consumer purchasing power on high fashion clothing and cosmetics in north China is even stronger than that of the South. Compared to people living south of the Yangtze River, northerners are much less likely to compare the price or quality of goods and services before making a prompt purchase decision.

Powerful Group Purchases for Non-productive Purposes

Group purchases in China are of two types: when an enterprise, company or other type of organisation buys equipment, raw materials, facilities, transportation or infrastructure in order to operate their business; and the purchase of non-productive consumer goods such as food, disposable commodities, houses, entertainment or holiday vouchers for employees. Since a Chinese enterprise is regarded as a type of small society, management is responsible for both the private and work lives of its employees.

Non-productive group purchases can include gifts, the cost of luxury hotel accommodation, and banquets for the purpose of business. For example, a company may buy admission to a private fishing pond, lake or stream as part of an entertainment package for its business partners or official supporters.

Non-productive group purchase is a general market phenomenon in China, characterised by vast buying power. According to a survey conducted by Chinese marketing statisticians, nearly one third of all consumer goods in the Chinese market is bought in this way. For this reason, for the Chinese central government an effective means of suppressing inflation is to limit non-productive group purchases by organisational or administrative means. For instance, it may issue a policy whereby the purchase of a particular non-productive item must be approved by the relevant governmental department.

The Purchasing Tendencies of Chinese Consumers

Chinese consumer characteristics have changed dramatically since 1978. In the 1970s the most sought-after items were bicycles, watches and sewing machines. In the 1980s it was television sets, washing machines and refrigerators. In the early 1990s it was video recorders and telephones.

Currently, computers, giant-sized television sets, air-conditioners and video cameras are the family purchasing priorities of most ordinary urban residents. Private housing and automobiles will be the purchasing targets of the future, with Beijing consumers favouring cars, and Shanghai consumers favouring homes. The explanation for this trend is that Beijing, being the capital of China, is where governmental departments, universities, research institutes and large central government-owned companies are located. In principle, these kinds of organisations should be able to provide their employees with housing. Many Beijing consumers who work in these organisations expect this, so housing is not their first purchasing priority. Accordingly, most people plan to use their savings to buy either a car or some other significant luxury item such as private-use multi-media technology. Shanghai, on the other hand, continues to have a housing supply problem. It is one of the most crowded cities in the world. For ordinary people the possibility of being allocated housing is slight, so they have to be prepared to save and buy their own home.

A Brief Introduction to Trends within the Chinese Market

Telecommunications Technology

Many foreign companies have contested China's telecommunication market since the early 1990s. It has been reported that at present there are on average 30 000 new household telephone installations every day. There were, for instance, 10 million telephones installed nationwide in 1994, and during this period total connections were twice the number of total existing telephones in Hong Kong. This has continued to grow with new installations at 12 million in 1996 and 21 million in 1997. In comparison, while possessing the largest actual number of telephones in the world, the greatest number of new connections in one year in the United States was only 7 million. China now outranks the USA in terms of the highest number of new telephone connections in any one recent year. In addition, in 1995 there were 3.6 million new mobile phone customers in China, and it is estimated that this number will swell to 18 million by the year 2000. In that case, China will soon be the largest telecommunications market in the world.

The Chinese Government has put a lot of time, effort and capital into a nationwide information-based scheme called 'The Three Golden Projects', which include:

- 'The Golden Customs Project': a national information network for domestic and international trade
- 'The Golden Tax Project': a national computer audit network
- 'The Golden Currency Project': a national system for coordinating electronic currency transfer.

Each project involves the development of telecommunications technology in government departments, educational institutions, banks and customhouses, commercial departments, tourism centres, industrial organisations and so on. This has created a large market for information technology products, and with it a number of 'golden' opportunities for foreign telecommunications companies. 'The Three Golden Projects' also involve trade in computers and software. Many foreign companies, like IBM, AT&T, Intel and others, have successfully cooperated with a number of Chinese enterprises to implement the goals of these projects.

The Personal Computer Market

According to 'The PRC [People's Republic of China] Desk Top PC Market Report of 1997', produced by the Huicong Group (the largest private marketing research company in China), the total selling volume of personal computers in China in the first half of 1997 was 1 431 000 units. The report estimates that China's annual selling PC volume will be over 3 000 000 units by the end of 1997, an increase of 61% on the previous year's total selling volume.

Table 7.1 Sales growth ranking of computer hardware of Chinese and foreign companies 1995–96

Company	Rank in 1996	Rank in 1995	Growth rate of sales (% annually)
Legend	1	4	144
IBM	2	3	78
Compaq	3	1	7
AST	4	2	12
HP	5	5	140
DEC	6	6	97
GW	7	7	83
Tong Chuang	8	9	189
Acer	9	8	133
Founder	10	10	–

Source: *China Computer Daily*, 1997.

The huge demand for personal computer technology in the Chinese market means substantial business opportunities for both Chinese and foreign companies. The total value of China's PC industry was estimated at 5 billion *RMB yuan* (about $US60 billion) in 1990. Five years later this had increased to 61.5 billion *RMB yuan* (about $US7.4365 billion). Multinational computer companies increased their sales in China accordingly, resulting in keen competition for market share. Table 7.1 indicates the sales growth ranking of computer hardware of both domestic and foreign companies in China between 1995 and 1996.

The Chinese Construction Material Market

The construction market is presently China's most important field of development. In the light of the Chinese government's 'Ninth National Five-Year Plan' (1996–2000), the size of an average urban dwelling should be 9m^2 per capita by the end of this century. To reach this low average standard living space, it is estimated that housing construction of 1.25 billion sqare metres is required given the present projection of 1.3 billion Chinese citizens by the end of this century. The Chinese Ministry of Construction has proposed that the following seven aspects of the construction and housing market are priorities for this industry from 1996:

- Kitchen and bathroom facilities
- Lightweight and flexible room or wall partitions
- Water and sewer pipe, and meters for water, electricity and gas
- High-quality doors and windows
- Home heating products, especially radiators
- Lighting and electrical facilities
- Insulating and indoor decorating materials.

Currently, the Chinese government encourages foreign companies and investors to cooperate with their Chinese counterparts to manufacture these types of goods for sale in China.

Automobile Market

Currently, on average there are 11.3 people for every one vehicle worldwide. However, in China this figure is about 109 people to one motor vehicle, and are approximately 900 persons to one motor car. Accordingly, the automobile industry is officially recognised as one of the most crucial developing industries in China. According to the Chinese Government, there will be 11–13 million families in China that can afford to buy car by the year 2000; 38 to 41 million by 2005; and 88 to 96 million by 2010. At this time China will constitute the largest automobile market in the world.

In 1997 the growth rate of privately purchased cars in China was 48.9%, just under half of the total market. At present, in China 200 000 *RMB yuan* (about US$20 400) is considered an acceptable price for a new car. According to the Chinese Customs Bureaux, China imported 82 000 vehicles in 1996, most manufactured in Germany, Japan, France, South Korea and the United States.

Interestingly, this was a 50% decrease on the 1995 figure. One of the reasons for this result was that many local governments stipulated a car-limiting policy. To achieve this, officials in different regions imposed a variety of duties on all cars. Many Chinese consumers can afford to buy a private motor vehicle but cannot afford the duty imposed after purchase. Due to governmental control and the current economic limitations, there was a high level of competition in the Chinese car market. Prices of various brands have subsequently fallen.

The Environmental Protection Market

The environmental protection industry is another priority of the Chinese Government, because China desperately needs to balance the needs of its enormous population with sustainable development and a clean environment. It is estimated that early in the next century, China will become the largest consumer of environmental protection products in the world. The Chinese Government has decided on an initial investment of $US450 billion in environmental protection from 1997 through to the year 2000. One hundred large or medium manufacturing enterprises that specialise in the production of environmental protection technology are now or will soon be under construction. However, in spite of the government's commitment, China's arduous environmental challenge and its acute lack of experience and expertise, as well as low capital and technology base, mean that a great deal of support will be required from foreign countries. Because of this, there are many business opportunities for foreign companies operating in this field. Chinese governmental statistics for 1995 indicated that profits in the environmental technology sector had risen 12.9% in one year.

Business Opportunities in Basic Industries

From 1980 through to 1997 the Chinese economy attracted total foreign investment of US$212.2 billion. Foreign investment allocation in China dictates that 50% of this investment capital is at present allocated to processing industries, 30% to tourism, real estate and hotel industries and 1.5 per cent to agriculture. Transportation, electricity and the oil and gas industry all together account for only 10% of total foreign investment. This indicates that during the past eight years foreigners have invested most of their capital in industries that require a minimum of capital but ensure a quick return, such as real estate. However, even with the rapid development of processing industries, technology, management and output, China's basic industries largely lag behind demand.

Therefore the Chinese central government has strengthened its commitment to the fundamentals of foreign investment in the National Ninth Five-Year Plan, through which the government intends to attract foreign investment into basic industries by providing investors with a set of 'most-favoured' policies. These areas or fields basically include new technology in agriculture, the development of synthetic soil resources, water conservation projects, raw material development, energy production, transportation infrastructure, telecommunications and, machinery upgrades, and finally the expansion of the electronic and mining industries. Consistent with this, the Chinese government issued two important policy directives in 1997. One was to give priority to developing the mid-west region of China through a 'most-favoured investment' policy for both foreign and domestic investors. Another was to provide foreign investors with set, transparent and predictable guidelines that focus on the projects most urgently required by China. Clearly it is in the best interests of all foreign investors to be familiar with the primary characteristics of the Chinese market and to understand the psychology that underpins this.

Chapter Eight

Promotion and Distribution in the Chinese Market

Effective promotion and distribution of goods and services are essential aspects of successful business in China. Culturally appropriate marketing research, the skills of promotion and branding, packaging and advertising from a Chinese cultural perspective are important aspects of establishing a distribution network in the Chinese market.

Marketing Research in China

The Necessity of Marketing Research

China is a market of 1.2 billion consumers, characterised by huge consumer demand. It is a market that has created almost incalculable business opportunities, mostly due to China's high level of economic growth, but also because of it close ties with international commerce. All these factors combine to make current and accurate commercial information the life-blood of the Chinese market.

China has a number of unique and exploitable consumer characteristics that exist in a relatively independent market, which is in the process of being transformed from an immature to a dynamic and unified system. Business is both attractive and risky. To reduce the risk of doing business to the lowest degree possible, comprehensive and effective marketing research is necessary before you contemplate entering China.

Obtaining relevant commercial data in China is a difficult task. First of all there is the problem of diverse ownership of the various entities. There are enormous differences in pricing systems and marketing channels, especially between state-owned and other types of enterprises. In contrast to Western developed countries, where enterprise data is available in publication or bulletin form, less than 20% of all Chinese enterprise data is available to the public or to relevant industry groups. Both the Chinese government and most state-owned organisations traditionally regard business information as classified, or rather as state secrets that must be protected at all costs.

Another problem is that the accounting systems of many Chinese companies, especially medium and small organisations, have not been completely standardised with international convention, chiefly because international standardised accounting practices were not introduced into China until the early 1990s. As a result, some accountants still do not hold formal qualifications. Consequently, accounting data may not accurately reflect a particluar firm's real financial situation. Therefore accounting data may be of little or no assistance to marketers or investors.

A fourth variable is that the Chinese market is immature and developing. Chinese consumers are facing accelerating change in most aspects of their lives. The introduction of new products and new ways of retailing in the context of increased incomes are constantly changing Chinese consumer values and behaviour.

The complication of disparate pricing and distribution systems, the lack of public commercial data, an undeveloped accounting system and changing consumer values all create obstacles to conducting meaningful marketing research. If you are planning to enter the Chinese market, is is essential that you hire professional Chinese marketing researchers to assist you.

Before the reforms of 1978, the State Statistics Bureau collected and then controlled most data about the Chinese market. Private marketing research companies in China did not appear until the late 1980s. Although there are currently many regional marketing consultative companies in China, only a few of these are permitted to or indeed have the capacity to conduct nationwide surveys and provide a standardised research report.

One exception is the Beijing's Huiecong Group, the largest private professional marketing research company in China, with over 40 subsidiaries and 1800 staff operating nation-wide. The Huiecong Group has developed a vast database that incorporates product quotation and marketing research with a comprehensive monitoring system. The Huiecong Group's international customers include many well-known companies such as IBM, Intel, Epson, Apc, Compaq, Philips, Farstar and Hewlett Packard.

Organising Marketing Research in China

Choosing a good marketing research or consultative organisation is a crucial first step. The market research company of choice should have a high profile and possess a nation-wide network. Ideally this company should have extensive experience in conducting surveys on behalf of multinational enterprises.

As a foreign client, you should ask the selected company to provide a detailed proposal and fee schedule. However, unlike in the West where consultancy proposals are free, in China a fee is charged. Your company must then sign an agreement with the Chinese consultative company to ensure that key goals are met. The items of agreement usually include research objectives, project scope and schedule, content of the report, cost and payment options, copyright, arbitration and confidentiality. Research quality control and standard of translation also need to be predetermined and incorporated into the contract. This is especially important if your company requires a time limitation on research and a final report in English. Large marketing research companies like the Huiecong Group are able to provide all of these, as well as international-standard, professional research consultancy:

- General market reports: this service covers sales volume, or the number of retailers and wholesalers of a certain product; the ranking of best seller, market analysis and product forecasts
- Analysis of the market structure according to specified dimensions: this may include trade structure, market share or technological specifications
- Analysis of the distribution of a brand or category of product or product
- Analysis of brand price and or profits
- Analysis of product end-users
- Analysis of the appearance rate of advertisements
- Analysis of the market investment environment.

Promotion in the Chinese Market

In the competitive Chinese market effective promotion makes the difference between market penetration and anonymity, so it is an essential ingredient of any successful sales formula.

Branding
Branding plays a very powerful role in the promotion of goods and services in the Chinese market. Most Chinese consumers

are brand-guided. The difference between consumer groups in China is that older consumers are more likely to be loyal to certain brands while middle-aged or younger consumers are more likely to pursue well-known, new or popular brands.

Branding in the Chinese market plays a promoting role different from that of other countries. In Western countries people pay more attention to how a brand name sounds when it is read aloud. On the other hand, the Chinese place a great deal of emphasis on the *meaning* of a brand word. This is culturally reflected in the following example. A baby boy in China may receive the name *Bowen*, which means that his parents hope that he will grow up to be knowledgeable in literature. A baby girl may be given the name *Lingyu*, which means that her parents wish her to be clever and beautiful. The same principle is true for choosing a brand name in Chinese business culture.

Chinese people choose a brand name according to both the meaning and the sound of a particular word, though in most circumstances meaning is more important than sound. Chinese businesspeople usually consider the meaning of a brand name from two perspectives. One is to attempt to directly tell the consumer how good their product is, or to inform them of the advantages of selecting their particular brand. For example, Chinese consumers have favourably responded to a brand of detergent called *Yixiling*, which means that 'clothes are made clean immediately on being touched by this particular brand of detergent'.

Another perspective on how and why a particular brand name is chosen is that a given brand may indicate that the product will bring the consumer 'a lucky result', 'good fortune' or 'best wishes'. For example, a brand of soap especially produced for older people is given the name *Zitian*, which in Mandarin means 'purple sandalwood'. In Chinese culture 'purple sandalwood' implies a very positive meaning, namely that old people are valued members of society, because many Chinese believe that the older a purple sandalwood plant is the stronger its fragrance. An expensive brand of man's shirts is called *Sheng-Shi*, meaning 'gentleman'. This brand's image implies a man of dignity and sophistication, and sells very well not just because it is a high quality article, but also because Chinese consumers feel very warm towards the actual brand name meaning.

In contrast, there are some imported goods which have attractive-sounding brand names in the language of their country of origin, but which are practically meaningless to a Chinese consumer. To counter this cultural ambiguity, Chinese marketers often attempt to confer a Chinese meaning on a particular foreign brand so that it can be understood and accepted by Chinese consumers. Translation of foreign brand names into Chinese can be flexible according to either the sound or the meaning of the original name. For example, the soft drink product 'Sprite', produced by the Coca-Cola Company, is translated into Chinese as *Xuebi*, basically according to its original sound, not according to its original meaning. Thus Chinese marketers carefully chose a new name with the same sound but with a special meaning. The word *Xuebi* in Chinese indicates a beautiful snowy scene filled with pristine ice crystals. This is intended to stimulate the Chinese consumers' imagination: the word's meaning makes people feel cool and comfortable in hot weather.

The brand name 'Coca-Cola' is translated as *Kekou Kele*, which means that the product is tasty and enjoyable. A brand of Swiss wristwatch called 'Radio' is translated as *Leida*, based on the sound of the original brand. *Leida* means 'radar', and is intended to convince Chinese consumers that this brand of watch is extremely accurate.

In the light of Chinese social sensitivities there are a number of branding principles that provide a reference point from which to design an appropriate and successful brand name. A brand intended for use by the older generation should relate to a meaning that indicates a particular health benefit. An appropriate brand name for a children's product should relate to intelligence or health. For men the best brand suggests a sense of blessing, good business, high status, financial success or luck. For women the most successful brand names are connected with beauty or youth.

Packaging

The important functions of packaging are to contain and protect the product, to promote the contents, and to facilitate storage for ease of delivery and finally for use. Of these, promotion is now the most important packaging function in China. Design, colours, shapes and packaging materials all have a powerful impact on consumer's perceptions and buying behaviour. This function had traditionally been ignored by Chinese manufacturers.

In the planned economy that existed before 1978, Chinese enterprises paid little attention to packaging aesthetics. Furthermore, they had no interest in finding out the consumers' point of view. Most product packaging was either out of date or out of fashion. Many were ugly. This weakened the competitive advantage of Chinese products in both the domestic and international market. After the implementation of the Open Door policy, changes in consumers' basic requirements, as well as market competition, forced Chinese enterprises to pay attention to packaging. In addition, foreign products featuring novel or elegant packaging provided a reference point for Chinese manufactures, particular after the 1980s when foreign goods poured into the Chinese market.

These influences have completely changed the way products are presented for sale in China. Chinese consumers' packaging requirements are now high, especially because of the custom of gift-giving, which demands that goods must appear both beautiful and valuable. Since in China it is not appropriate to open a gift in public, the gift-giver must ensure that the packaging accurately reflects the contents, so that everyone who witnesses the presentation will be impressed. So the primary social function of packaging is to give the receiver 'face', and in return the gift-giver also gains 'face'. Chinese consumers are therefore willing to pay a high price for a product with elegant packaging. There have been many examples in the Chinese market where the sales of a particular product have increased dramatically after being presented in a more attractive manner. Of two brands of the same quality, the one with the most impressive packaging will command the higher price and the higher sales volume in the Chinese market. A product with an intrinsically high value is hardly recognised by Chinese customers if its packaging design style looks plain.

Foreign companies who wish to sell their products in China must pay careful attention to this important cultural trait. For instance, two vintages of imported wine appeared in the Beijing market in 1995. One was produced in Australia, the other in France. At the time many Chinese consumers were aware that both France and Australia were two of the most famous wine-producing countries in the world. However, respective sales of the two vintages were significantly different—the French wine outsold the Australian wine by many times. In terms of price there was not much difference between the two competitors, but their packaging varied considerably. The former was packed in a slender and refined box that looked both notable and grand, and conveyed the impression that the contents were at least as good as the packaging. This brand became famous. Beijing consumers quickly fell in love with this particular wine, and it remained the market leader for many years. One important reason for this success was that Chinese consumers regard the French wine as one of the most impressive options for gift-giving because it is so beautifully presented.

The Australian wine was of a similarly high standard, but the way it was presented was ordinary and pedestrian. It attracted very little attention and was quickly overlooked by the Chinese consumer. The Australian wine was marketed in single unpackaged bottles, unlike its elaborately boxed French competitor. The Australian marketing representative had gone to a great deal of trouble to keep his product price-competitive by eliminating expensive packaging. For Chinese consumers, wine or indeed any other alcoholic drink that is not packaged in an elegant box, festooned with lace, is unsuitable as a gift. Under normal circumstances, ordinary Chinese consumers are not willing to spend very much on expensive goods for their own consumption, but feel that it is worth paying extra to successfully fulfil the social requirements of gift-giving. As a result, at that time Australian wines could not compete with French wines in the Beijing market.

It has been said that Chinese people like the colour red in packaging. Nowadays, this comment is only partially true. Chinese consumers choose goods with red packaging when they want to give a wedding gift, as a present to the aged, or for their own consumption in some traditional Chinese festivals. For Chinese people the colour red looks both joyous and lucky. Nevertheless, they may select different-coloured packaging for different reasons at different times. For example, many young women in China prefer 'magnificent colours' for the packaging of clothes or cosmetics. Only the colour dark blue must still be used with caution in packaging, because Chinese consumers, especially old people, sometimes identify it with death.

Changing tastes in colour preference can been seen in China's modern-day wedding ceremony. In the old days, a Chinese bride would wear only red to her wedding. Nowadays, most brides wear various sets of clothes in different colours, especially in urban areas where consumer demand and awareness are high. In fact a modern Chinese bride may wear several sets of new clothes at different times during the ceremony. A bride's change of clothes includes a traditional red wedding dress, Western-style wedding clothes in pure white and an array of fashionable clothes in various colours.

As a final note, the Chinese Commercial Department stipulates that all product labels must contain a detailed description of the product, including the address of the producer and place of manufacture. Labels on imported products must be in legible Chinese.

Advertising

Media categories

The strategic use of media is one of the most important aspects of effective business in China. The official media has a powerful impact on the Chinese people. Due to the political system, the government controls the media nationwide, though to a lesser extent in the regional areas. In particular, national media are tightly controlled and supervised by the Propaganda Department of the CCP, the Ministry of Radio, Film and Television of the State Council, and the State News Publishing

Bureau. Since the Chinese media are financed by the government, they are ranked as government organisations.

China's media groupings are normally categorised into four types, based on their administration.

Media administered by the central government: Many media organisations like the China Central Television Station (CCTV), the China Central Radio Station (CCRS), the China News Agency, the Xinyuan News Agency, *The People's Daily* and *The Qiushi Magazine* are directly administered by the central government. These media enjoy massive audiences: their readers, listeners and viewers have a powerful influence on Chinese business practice. For instance, almost 300 million people watch CCTV every day. *The People's Daily*, which is run by the CCP, has an equally extensive distribution, as every local branch of the CCP across China subscribes.

Unlike in some Western countries, where government-operated media limit the transmission of commercial advertisements, all of these media are allowed to display commercials in China. Advertising fees for CCTV are usually higher than other forms of Chinese media because CCTV broadcasts nationwide, even worldwide. It also enjoys a very high profile among the Chinese people. Television is usually the first option for promotion for companies that possess a China-wide distribution network and have deep pockets. The effectiveness of promotion in this media category in China is pre-eminent.

Media administered by the ministries, and provincial and municipal governments: In China, ministries of the central government, provincial governments and city administrations with provincial status administer some media organisations directly. Every province and municipality under the direct control of the central government has their own television station, radio station and at least one newspaper. The influence of these media mostly covers provincial or individual city areas. However, with the development of a satellite system in China, some of these television and radio stations can now broadcast their programmes to other provinces. For instance, Beijing receives programmes broadcast by television stations in Shanghai, the Tibet Autonomous Region, Yuennian Province, and so on.

Many of the central government ministries operate their own newspapers, focusing on their own particular professional fields. Currently these include:

- *The Guangming Daily* (run by the State Education Commission)
- *The Economy Daily* (run by State Economic and Trade Commission)
- *The Legal Daily* (run by Ministry of Justice)
- *The Science and Technology Daily* (run by the State Science and Technology Commission)
- *The China Business Times* (run by the China Federation of Industry and Business)
- *The Sports Daily* (run by the State Physical Culture and Sports Commission).

These newspapers not only cater for professional groups, but are also distributed across China for general readership.

These particular publications are less controlled by the central government, so their news reports or regular columns are a little more flexible. Most papers and TV stations in this category are very popular among both local and provincial readers and audiences. For example, *The China Business Times*, *The Beijing Evening*, *The Yangcheng Evening* (in Guangzhou City), *The Xinmin Evening* (Shanghai City), Beijing Television, Orient Television (Shanghai City) and Guangdou Television are very popular both locally and provincially. Advertising fees are lower than for centrally controlled media, as their broadcast or distribution coverage area is smaller, being more focused on specific audiences or readership groups. They are more suitable for advertisements promoting products in certain specialised geographical or professional fields of interest.

Media administered by municipal or county governments: Every municipal and county government in China operates a television station, radio network or newspaper or papers. These media are the primary means by which local residents obtain news and information, including details of local job recruitment. Movies, documentaries and drama series occupy most of the broadcasting time in these TV stations. These media are an effective means of promoting products in local regions only. Advertising rates are of course lower than in metropolitan areas.

Media administered by large state-owned enterprises: In China, many state-owned enterprises employ over several thousand workers each. The population of one enterprise may total 100 000 (if employees' families are counted as well). Being like a small society, they not only have their own hospital, school, shops, sports facilities and child care centres, but also have their own television station, radio network, and newspaper or papers. The main purpose of these local media is to provide employees and their families with information about their particular enterprise's activities and organisational work performance. These outlets also sell advertising, though the quality of advertising is not as high as those in the other categories. However, enterprise-based television, radio and newspapers can be a useful means of promotion if you want to explore the market of a particular target community. The advantages are that they are popular with local residents; the rate of watching, listening or reading is high; and the advertising tariffs are low.

In summary, although they are all financed by the government and no purely commercially run media exist, all the various forms and categories of China's media are allowed to engage in commercial advertising. Such advertising has been one of the main sources of revenue for many government enterprises in the media industry, because the government's financial allocation is far from adequate to allow them to run effectively. Communication enterprises such as CCTV actually depend on advertising income to maintain their operations. They also depend on advertising revenue to provide employees with various forms of basic welfare.

The development of China's advertising industry
With the increase in the number of media outlets, China's advertising industry has developed in leaps and bounds. For most

enterprises, advertising has already become the main means of promotion.

Before the Open Door reforms, there were 53 television stations in China. By 1995, however, there were 3125, an increase of 60 times from 1977. The current number is 10 times as many as the number of television stations in the United States; 25 times as many as the number in Japan; and 260 times as many as the number of British stations. The growth rate of stations across China and the government's positive encouragement of advertising have facilitated the development of the world's most dynamic advertising industry.

The first commercial advertisement on Chinese television was broadcast at 6.59 p.m. (in prime time just before the evening news program on CCTV) on 15 March 1979. Since then, the advertising industry has been growing at the rate of 40% each year, 30% higher than the average growth rate of China's overall economy. According to one report, the turnover of China's advertising industry was respectively 20 billion *RMB yuan* (about US$2.413 billion) in 1994, 30 billion *RMB yuan* (about US$3.628 billion) in 1995, and up to 38 billion *RMB yuan* (about US$ 4.59 billion) in 1996.

China's first Advertising Act became effective on 1 July 1995. The advertising industry in China has since enjoyed constant official support through the reform of commercial law relating to advertising and promotion. For example, CCTV first implemented a policy that the advertising fee for 'golden time' (i.e. prime time, from 7.30 p.m. to 7.35 p.m. right after the evening news) should be auctioned to the highest bidder. This means that the advertising fee for 'golden time' on CCTV has no fixed price. The advertiser who pays the highest price gets their advertisement displayed on prime-time CCTV. Some foreign advertising experts have claimed that the growth of China's advertising industry is like a 'reinless horse', and estimate that China will become the largest advertising market in the world by the year 2010.

Rates for foreign enterprises advertising on CCTV, effective
from 1997 (see Table 8.1), provide a reference point for the
highest television advertising rates in China. The 1997 advertising rates for *The Financial Times*, *The China Business Times*, *The
Wen-Hie Daily* and *The Yang Cheng Evening* (see Table 8.2) also
provide a rough reference rate for newspaper advertising
tariffs.

Table 8.1 Rates for foreign product advertising on CCTV
(Effective from 1 January 1997)

Categories		Time	Price for 15 seconds (US$)		Price for 30 seconds (US$)	
			Mon–Thurs	Fri–Sun	Mon–Thurs	Fri–Sun
Channel Two	A	6–9 p.m.	10 000	11 000	16 000	17 000
	B	9–10 p.m.	9 000	10 000	15 000	16 000
	C	After 10 p.m.	7 000	8 000	12 000	13 000
Channel Eight			5 000		8 000	
Channel Fifteen			2 500		4 000	
Channel Thirty-two			2 000		3 200	
Channel Thirty-three			1 200		1 900	

Commission: 15%
Source: Advertising Department, CCTV (1997).

Table 8.2 Some newspaper advertising rates

Advertise- ment size in black and white	The Financial Times (Beijing, nationwide)	The China Business Times (Beijing, nationwide)	The Wen-Hie Daily (Shanghai, nationwide)	The Yang- Cheng Eve- ning (Guangzhou)
12×17 (or 17.5) cm (2nd or 4th page)	17 000 RMB	12 000 RMB	—	31 100 RMB
12×35 cm or 24×17.5 cm (2nd or 4th page)	28 000 RMB	25 000 RMB	38 000 RMB	31 100 RMB

Promotion and Distribution in the Chinese Market

Advertise-ment size in black and white	The Financial Times (Beijing, nationwide)	The China Business Times (Beijing, nationwide)	The Wen-Hie Daily (Shanghai, nationwide)	The Yang-Cheng Evening (Guangzhou)
24r35 cm (2nd or 4th page)	60 000 RMB	44 000 RMB	72 500 RMB	136 860 RMB
49×35 cm (2nd or 4th page)	100 000 RMB	88 000 RMB	145 000 RMB	285 110 RMB

Sources: Advertising Department, *The Financial Times* (1997); Advertising Department, *The China Business Times* (1997); Advertising Department, *The Wen-Hei Daily* (1996); Advertising Department, *The Yang-Cheng Evening* (1997).

Significantly, foreign companies operating in China or registered joint ventures are usually required to pay up to twice as much for advertising than Chinese customers do.

The Role of Public Relations in Promotion

The concept of public relations, according to the Western theory and strategic practice of establishing a good corporate image, has been extremely popular in China since 1987. However, when it was first introduced into China, most businesspeople and managers misunderstood the concept. They regarded public relations as a procedure whereby personal relationship networks were established in order to facilitate the attainment of corporate goals. This misunderstanding may have resulted from a particular cultural or educational background or from direct work experience in state-owned enterprises. Influenced by the Chinese value of 'relationship orientation', Chinese businesspeople confused 'public relations' with guanxi or 'connections', culturally already well-accepted in Chinese business.

Secondly, in the late 1980s, demand outstripped supply in the Chinese market, especially for raw materials and financial resources, which were tightly controlled by a small number of powerful individuals within specific government departments. This situation led Chinese businesspeople and managers to focus on the relationship between their enterprise, officials and suppliers, instead of the relationship between their enterprise and suppliers, customers, employees and other related organisations. The deeper reason for this was that under China's centrally planned economy, enterprises decided what consumers wanted and then only produced what they believed they needed.

With the development of China's economy since the 1990s, a sellers' market has turned into a buyers' market. Chinese managers and businesspeople have been forced to accept the concept of market competition, and have had to agree that consumer demand should now drive production. Nowadays, the fate of most enterprises is decided by its competitive capacity. To this extent the focus is now on the consumer, at least in the minds of many managers (although personal relationships with officials and other businesspeople are still recognised as crucial to success in business). Subsequent to the mid-1990s, 'public relations' has been correctly reinterpreted by Chinese managers and businesspeople. According to their current understanding, public relations is an important marketing tool which assists enterprises in building up a good public or corporate profile.

Many Chinese enterprises and companies, including state-owned, collective-owned, or private enterprises, have set up public relations departments, whose main task is to communicate with the public, solve conflicts between the enterprise and customers, to report information about public demand to top management, and to assist management in deciding on correct marketing strategies. These departments are now referred to as 'the creators of the enterprise image'. At present, there are four types of public relations activities operating in China.

Publicity-oriented public relations
Publicity-oriented public relations focuses on publishing and promoting the image of a particular enterprise in the public forum through various types of media. Qualified Chinese public relations managers often have good connections with the media, having worked as either journalists or editors before taking up their position. They are capable of and responsible for channelling and maintaining a good working relationship with their

previous colleagues. They make use of these relationships to frequently report information about their enterprise in the form of 'soft' advertising in order to highlight its public profile.

Socially oriented public relations

Socially oriented public relations focuses on establishing extensive business networks with key social players. Since Chinese business culture places a high premium on relationships based on personal friendship, on many occasions informal relationships are more effective than formal ones in helping to find solutions to particular management problems. As in any business culture anywhere, a good public relations manager must possess a high degree of communication and interpersonal skills. This makes the job of a public relations manager in China not only very complicated but also very subtle. They must be able to organise a wide variety of public and private activities, such as business openings, anniversary celebrations, and the introduction of a new product or product line to the market. In order to raise a particular company's corporate profile, a good public relations manager must be able to ensure the participation of a broad range of important guests such as officials and customers. Suppliers, other businesspeople, local and regional officials, bankers, representatives of the Price Bureau, the Tax Office, and the Department of Administration of Industry and Commence, must all be invited to the appropriate reception, banquet or opening. They must also be included in any recreational activity that is organised by the public relations manager for the benefit of foreign guests. Each and every relevant person must be contacted in an appropriate way with a minimum of cost to the enterprise.

Consultative public relations

Consultative public relations focuses on the analysis of information and data. It provides management with public feedback about the enterprise's product and image. In China consultative public relations usually includes activities such as customer-focused professional sales and marketing seminars, as well as the evaluation of questionnaire-survey results or complaints.

'Public good' oriented public relations
The 'public good' oriented type of public relations is designed
to raise the profile of an enterprise by sponsoring various public welfare activities. For both individual businesspeople and
their respective organisations, a good reputation is paramount.
Businesspeople or enterprises take part in such philanthropic
activities for reasons besides effectively promoting their product. Chinese business culture emphasises the value of 'face'.
Business people and enterprises will feel a sense of shame if
they are identified as being stingy, so a show of public generosity 'wins face'. In addition, some businesspeople in China are
still worried about the traditional value which maintains that
business is basically immoral. In this way businesspeople try to
redress a negative impression of their company by engaging in
charitable activities.

In these cases, many non-profit or non-business organisations
take advantage of these values to seek sponsorship from large
projects through organising social activities intended to have a
strong and positive influence on public opinion. A medium or
large enterprise may receive a great number of various sponsorship invitations every day. These non-profit organisations may
be governmental or non-governmental, or may be primary or
secondary schools or universities. A local government authority
may ask an enterprise to be the sponsor of a bridge or other
construction project. The reward for this support is often nam-
ing rights. Not surprisingly, sporting organisations in China are
almost all sponsored by enterprises.

In China there are always too many invitations for enterprises
to donate money to establish good corporate citizenship credentials. Enterprises have difficulty donating money to them
all, and so risk causing disappointment, thereby losing 'face'.
For very practical reasons, China's State Council has stipulated
that an enterprise has the right to reject any sponsorship demand. However, sometimes enterprises are 'forced' to take part
in public welfare activities even though they do not have their
hearts in it. They must, however, often agree to support certain
charitable projects because of concerns about 'face' protection
and- v long-term personal relationships. Hence, there is a com-

mon saying in Chinese public relations circles that 'The best and brightest public relations expert is not the one who can satisfy all sponsorship demands, but is the one who can maintain a good relationship with others even after rejecting their demand for sponsorship'.

Currently, public relations in China are considered a general managerial practice. China's rapidly changing market and complicated political and social systems suggest that qualified public relations managers are in demand. An expert public relations manager must understand the characteristics of the Chinese market, be able to establish friendly relationships with various governmental departments and the media, and possess experience, professional knowledge and skills in a wide range of interpersonal activities. Although it is easy to find skilled workers in China, it is very difficult to recruit qualified managers, including managers of public relations. An enterprise would consider itself extremely fortunate if it could attract a senior or experienced public relations manager, since public relations plays a key role in successful business in China.

'Hard' and 'Soft' Advertisements

In China, media promotion appears in two forms. One form is completely commercial, referred to by the Chinese as 'hard advertising'. 'Hard advertising', like most commercial advertising in the West, is designed and produced to promote a particular product or enterprise image. The advertising agency is responsible for negotiating with the media to arrange all advertising details: broadcasting time, news column space etc. Most Chinese advertising agencies charge a fee for design and production, and also charge the media organisation a 10% to 15% agency fee. Advertising charges are based on market prices. China's Advertising Act stipulates that any enterprise wishing to advertise its product or service must show its business licence and product qualifications to both the advertising agency and the media.

Another type of advertisement referred to by Western marketing theory as 'publicity' is favourable information about a company, goods or services that appears in the mass media as a news item. Chinese people refer to this type of advertisement as 'soft advertising'. Chinese enterprise public relations managers may provide journalists with a certain kind of benefit or convenience in appreciation for their cooperation, and in return the journalists will be expected to guarantee to report information in the form of a news story. In the reported story, information about the enterprise, including management, technology and production capacity, are covered in detail. Naturally the nature, characteristics and advantages of the particular enterprise's goods or services are indirectly promoted.

Under certain circumstances, Chinese businesspeople prefer 'soft advertising'. Compared with 'hard advertising', it has some distinct advantages. It easily wins the trust of most Chinese consumers. Audiences and readers feel that a news report published in the media is based on facts and contains less commercial overstatement about products. 'Soft advertising' can not only promote goods and services, but can also effectively and positively raise the image of a particular enterprise. Due to the competitiveness of the Chinese market, the image of an enterprise is having more and more attention paid to it by management circles. Additionally, the cost of providing benefits to journalists for 'soft' advertising' is much less than that of 'hard advertising'.

Organising good publicity can be expensive. In developed countries, although an organisation does not necessarily have to pay for mass media exposure, preparing press releases and persuading media personalities to print or broadcast their news items does take resources and does cost money. The same is even truer in China. Publicity, or more correctly 'soft advertising', in China is not free. Sometimes it may be very costly, especially if a Chinese enterprise wants to select the media which will display it. Time or space resources in the media in China, particularly in popular newspapers and television channels, remain in extremely short supply. Furthermore, newspapers with a nationwide distribution cannot offer one single additional page for publication without China's State Administration of News, Press and Publication first granting permission to do so. Chinese journalists and editors are in a very powerful position to decide what news and which stories should be reported. They can easily refuse to report information about an enterprise that is keen to demand publicity. This is one of the reasons why it is important to have a good relationship with the department or departments of the media and with journalists.

Benefits for journalists and/or editors could be an amount of money, or the use of goods or services in kind, banquets, or travel etc. Actually, a journalist who obtains benefit for reporting a particular story is violating official regulations, but their low income puts them in a position where they are quickly tempted to compromise. Some journalists' incomes from unofficial sources may be higher than from their formal salaries.

Approximately 1000 TV series or documentaries are produced in China annually. Among them only a few are sponsored by the government. The production of most of these series and documentaries relies on sponsorship, of which Chinese enterprises and companies are the main sources. These programmes are seen as effective ways of promoting the profile of organisations and sometimes their products. Programme sponsorship is also categorised as 'soft advertising' by the Chinese commercial community.

The following example demonstrates the effectiveness of 'soft advertising' on Chinese consumers.

A company which produced a brand of mineral water receptacle was nearly bankrupt in 1991 because it could not sell its product in the Chinese market. A 'soft' advertising campaign saved this enterprise. As the sponsor of a television comedy series, this firm's product was deliberately used in the series by the filmmaker. The comedy became very popular across China, and so did the product whose sales increased dramatically.

Of course, product placement is very common in the West too, both on TV and in the cinema.

The influence of advertising to promote the profile, product and service of enterprises in China is extremely powerful. This is related to Chinese consumer psychology and to the high profile that most forms of media enjoy among Chinese audiences. Since the government basically administrates China's media, especially television, radio and important newspapers, ordinary Chinese trust most reports about commerce or trade as long as these stories are presented as 'official news'. The relevant departments of the Chinese Government at different levels frequently check agencies and organisations involved in the advertising industry against the terms and conditions of the Advertising Act. The relatively strict control of the Chinese Government over the advertising industry reinforces ordinary people's sense of trust in the media.

The Chinese consumer psychology of 'vying for purchasing' is the other element that contributes to the effectiveness of advertising in China. Information in the form of television advertisements plays a powerful role.

An alcoholic drink named *Kong-fu JiaJiu* (which means 'a spirit specially made in the Confucian Mansion') was one of many almost unknown brands of liqueur on the Chinese market in the early 1990s. Older and well-established brands like *Maotai, Wulyang Ye* and *Luzhou Daqu* totally dominated market share at that time. However, the producers of this liqueur wisely decided to promote the product through an intensive advertising campaign. The company borrowed a large amount of money to finance advertising on the best television channel in China, CCTV, during 'golden time'—the fee for this campaign was about 100 million *RMB yuan* (about US$12 million). From this time on, however, *Kong-fu JiaJiu* has continually advertised on CCTV, spending about 100 million *RMB yuan* a year (about US$12 million), resulting in amazing success. *Kong-fu JiaJiu* is now the market leader in its field.

Distribution in the Chinese Market

Current Distribution Conditions

In China before the late 1970s, the distribution of all goods was completely controlled by the government according to a central plan. Since the Open Door policy, China's distribution channels have been improved dramatically, decentralised among thousands of new independent dealers. Most industrial products and commodities, with the exception of some important agricultural products, are distributed according to market demand and priced by dealers themselves. However, despite this very positive development, distribution in China at present still cannot be compared favourably with other more developed countries. Cross-country distribution networks remain undeveloped, with regional blockades effectively hampering the free flow of certain goods into some territories. In addition, national infrastructure remains relatively undeveloped, which results in the charging of relatively high delivery fees outside metropolitan centres.

Inefficient distribution systems

China has always had a traditional distribution system, a loose network of local dealers scattered throughout the country, though it was very inefficient. There are only a few new wholesaling or nationwide markets in China. These include the wholesale market of small commodities in Yi Wu City in Zhejiang Province, the wholesaling vegetable market in Rong Cheng City in Shan-dong Province and the steel and metal exchange market in Shanghai. The number of these primary wholesaling networks across China is far from satisfactory for either producers or end users.

China is actually not one market but several. Regional trade blockades exist in many areas and territories across China. Due to uneven development of the economy in different areas, many local officials and businesspeople have a strong sense of protecting their own regional trade interests. Local governments sometimes issue particular policies to ban certain goods from being 'imported' into their territory. For instance, a beer producer in Shan-Dong Province wanted to sell its product to people in a neighbouring city with a population of 8 million, only 150 kilometres away in Jiang-Su Province. However, the municipal government issued a ban to block the sale of 'imported' beer. Their excuse was that different provinces each have their own administrative affiliations with industry within the system, and should not become involved with business that does not concern them.

In order to establish more effective nationwide marketing networks, the central government has used administrative means to limit the negative influence of regional trade protectionism. At the same time, it has encouraged the development of 'chain trade'. Since 1992, a few of China's largest companies have established a national distribution chain, although they still have not gained access to all major Chinese territories. This problem remains for both logistical and political reasons.

Distribution channel conflict

Vertical distribution conflict easily occurs between manufacturers and retailers in China. Currently, the Chinese market is very competitive, with both costs and sales increasing. In the main cities of Beijing, Shanghai and Guangzhou, retailers generally charge about 30%, or even up to 40%, of the actual sale price. There is an unwritten rule in the Beijing market that retailers usually do not pay a trade invoice until three months after the goods have been sold. Retailers may sometimes also further delay payment or return of unsold stock because of difficulty in turnover. Conflicts of this nature may also cause the breakdown of established distribution channels.

Infrastructure problems

Current infrastructure facilities for the distribution and delivery of goods and services in China remain in an unsatisfactory condition, particularly in the transport industry. As a result, the delivery cost of products is relatively expensive, and delivery time over long distances is slow. For instance, in 1997 hauling a shipping container 1800 km from Shanghai to Guangzhou cost US$0.55/km and took 43 hours. Realising the limitations of China's inadequate infrastructure, the government will spend up to $US500 billion over the next three years to upgrade the infrastructure, particularly in the key transport sector where inadequate road, rail and postal delivery facilities are commonplace.

Establishment of Marketing Channels

Because of these negative factors, the establishment of effective marketing channels is one of the greatest challenges for both Chinese and foreign marketers. Accordingly, if you intend to distribute your product in China, take the following points as references when attempting to design a marketing channel.

Firstly, a distribution channel network must concentrate on building up bases in three to five large cities where commerce is already highly developed. The network can then be expanded to other cities after initial success. From a Chinese business tactic point of view, the saying is 'Go ahead steadily and strike sure blows'. During the procedure of building up bases of distribution, you can obtain experience and skills in operating a marketing channel network in China. This presents an opportunity to sound out the opinion of Chinese consumers, which in turn will provide important information about future growth rates and distribution expansion. Areas covered by expanded distribution must be carefully taken into account in order to reduce delivery cost. We strongly advise selecting areas for market expansion that are near the original distribution point.

Secondly, having a good relationship with local dealers and a degree of financial strength are two of the most important preconditions for selecting distribution channel members in China. The Chinese market is so large that a single producer cannot possibly manage distribution throughout the entire country. You need to make use of relationships—*guanxi*—with local dealerships to develop your market share in an effective way. Xerox of Shanghai, for example, has used this to dramatically increase its sales across China. It credits much of its 43% market share in China to the friendships that were developed over time by local dealers. An agent or company with a high profile, wide network and strong financial strength is able to help a Chinese or foreign manufacturer develop their market promptly.

Thirdly, besides the distribution channels, there are a number of specific outlets. Speciality stores are one of the best sales pathways in China. Apart from an increasing number of retailers, department stores, plazas and speciality stores appeal very much to Chinese consumers. Some well-known foreign fashion designers and producers have succeeded in China through the use of these outlets. Children's, men's and women's clothing and other luxury merchandise can be sold more effectively in speciality stores than in other types of retail outlets, because some Chinese consumers, such as the young or the wealthy, prefer to purchase well-known, fashionable or 'trendy' brands. Speciality stores can easily establish a particular brand among Chinese consumers who are otherwise swamped with competing merchandise.

Finally, supply conferences and exhibitions in China are helpful in establishing successful and lasting distribution networks.

Chapter Nine

How to Do Business Successfully in China
The Key Points

According to a 1997 World Bank report, China is at an economic crossroads. One turn in the road could lead to unprecedented commercial success. This, the World Bank states, is dependent on the Chinese Government's continued reform programme, especially in the areas of good administration and sound economic policy. A wrong turn in China's 'path to glory' could result in a catastrophe, especially if the fundamentals of Deng Xiao Ping's Open Door policy are rejected and China again closes its doors to the international community.

The same report lists China's strengths as its high savings rate, pragmatic economic reforms, relative stability, disciplined and literate labour force and growing administrative capacity. In addition, it points out that China enjoys a great deal of support from ethnic Chinese scattered outside China—its 'diaspora'. These strengths, combined with a massive market and highly competitive wage rates, make China a very attractive place to do business. Currently there are many foreign companies enjoying steady profitable growth in the Chinese market, largely due to their company's extensive knowledge of China's unique business culture as well as their local experience in marketing and sales.

However, for those who do not know how to deal with the cultural, legal, economic and political differences between China and the West, business in China can pose substantial risks. The World Bank's report also warns: 'Impressive as China's strengths are, they do not guarantee success.' It goes on to say that 'the risks and challenges are strong and varied enough to seriously threaten progress'. The report sites corruption, for example, as one of China's greatest challenges, and a major disincentive to foreign investment.

For these reasons, you must fully prepare yourself before entering the Chinese market. This includes evaluating the necessity of taking strategic risks. In China, as in any country, the business rule of thumb is that the higher the risk, the greater the return. In weighing up the risks and the benefits of participating in the world's largest market, you must possess the 'Six P's': patience, power, predisposition, personnel, protection and perspective.

The Six P's

Patience: Psychological Preparation

If you are to successfully invest capital, establish a joint venture or sell products in the Chinese market, you must be patient. It takes time to succeed in the Chinese business environment. Foreign businesspeople who expect to gain an immediate return on their capital or infrastructure investment in China will be disappointed.

The Chinese market is huge but immature, so it takes a long time for foreigners to establish a strong business base. In the first instance this is due to a number of negative factors: trade protectionism exists in many regions across China; the administrative system of official regulations is underdeveloped; the current progressive changes in Chinese commercial law have not yet been completely implemented; and some Chinese businesspeople increase the risk to foreigners by not following the unwritten rules of business.

Chinese businesspeople also have to adapt themselves to these factors, including corrupt business behaviour. A survey conducted by the *Wenhiu Daily* sheds some light on the Chinese manager's tolerance of immoral conduct in commerce. Clearly overcoming corruption in China will be a long process.

Table 9.1 Chinese managers' tolerance to immoral behaviour in commercial activities

Types of immoral behaviour	*Degree of tolerance*
Bribery of persons in charge	79.8%
Bribing customers	71.3%
Underweighting goods for sale	55.45%
Dishonest advertising	55.0%
Evading taxation	18.35%
Environmental pollution	3.3%

Source: *Wenhiu Daily*, 14 March 1997

Secondly, the Chinese market is very hard to anticipate. Due to continuous reform in every area of industry, values and incomes are changing, resulting in constant change to individual purchasing power and buying behaviour. At the same time, the Chinese market is bitterly competitive. As China's domestic market opens up to foreign competition, an enormous variety of commodities has been offered to consumers, each with its own domestic and imported competitors and all competing in quality, presentation and price. Because of this, Chinese consumers have plenty of options to consider before making a purchasing decision, so it is a difficult task to introduce a new product to the Chinese market and even more difficult to ensure its popularity. It takes time and an effective level of promotion for the consumer to first recognise and then select a new product. Of course huge profits will flow once a brand becomes popular.

Thirdly, government policy has a strong impact on the development of commerce in China. A particular industry or foreign business sometimes needs to be patient and wait for supportive policies to be issued, or rather developed. The Chinese government's Open Door policy is making great progress towards changing what was before 1978 a centrally planned economy. Nevertheless, the government still controls the market. Government policy may lead to the granting of concessions, or it may place obstacles in the way of domestic or foreign business. Unfortunately they are often changed, adjusted or reformed at short notice, and sometimes these changes have a negative impact on certain aspects of business.

An example of this can be found in the Chinese Government's 'favoured' policy towards foreign investment in the Chinese beer industry. Beer consumption in China has been growing at about 20% annually since the late 1980s—it is estimated that China will become the world's largest beer market in the near future. Appropriately, many foreign beer producers recognised the growth potential of this market and established a number of joint or wholly owned commercial ventures. Something of a trade war ensued between competing foreign interests on the one hand and between foreign and domestic beer producers on the other. In this war, domestic Chinese beer producers suffered immediate and substantial loss. Soon afterwards, for the sake of protecting the domestic beer industry, the government made a number of 'policy adjustments': from 1996 onwards the Chinese government decided to limit the operations of foreign beer producers in the Chinese market. This modified policy caused substantial short-term loss for foreign investors. Because international beer companies had correctly planned ahead by investing substantial financial resources into promotion, advertising, distribution infrastructure and increased production capacity, their loss was great. This new protectionism may only be a temporary deviation from a longer-term view, but according to some foreign beer producers the damage has already been done.

Another example concerns investment in the importation of capital equipment for infrastructure development in China-based, foreign-owned or joint-venture manufacturing plants. Since the first days of the Open Door reforms, foreign investors have enjoyed a duty-free status on the importation of equipment and technology. This policy successfully attracted an enormous amount of foreign investment. Unfortunately, in 1996 the central government suddenly announced that this policy was to be overturned. However, after one year it was found that the cancellation of this particular policy was a disaster—foreign capital flow had immediately dropped off, producing an immediate and negative impact on the Government's industrial modernisation programme. The Chinese Government resumed the policy again on 1 January 1998.

A very strong signal was sent to the international commercial community that the Chinese government was prepared, if necessary, to move the goal posts when it suited them, but then they were also prepared to put the goal posts back. Clearly a long-term view and patience are necessary prerequisites of doing business in China.

Power: Financial Strength

Running a successful business in China requires strong financial power. The Chinese market is like an ocean: a business with weak financial power is like a small boat that can easily be capsized in economic bad weather, while a business with great financial strength is like an ocean-going supertanker that can resist even the roughest conditions. Practice and analysis has shown that entering the Chinese market requires very deep pockets. Initial profits are elusive until you learn to adapt to the subtleties of Chinese business culture and the realities of the Chinese market, including determining how much capital is required to promote goods or services.

The costs associated with exploring the Chinese market are relatively high. Some business expenses in China are higher than in many Western countries. Advertising fees and office rental, for example, are among the highest in the world. Table 9.2 shows the cost of office rental in Beijing for 1997.

Table 9.2 Office rental, Beijing in 1997

Office location	Rental rate	Rental terms
International Centre	US$70/m² per month	2-year minimum term
Beijing Holiday Inn	US$60/m² per month	1-year minimum term
Cheng Li Palace Hotel	US$60/m² per month	2-year minimum term
Yan Sha Centre	US$60/m² per month	2-year minimum term
Standard room as an office in the Great Wall Hotel (five-star)	US$110 plus 15% service fee per day	6-month minimum term

In China advertising rates or rental fees have a direct relationship to business opportunities. The promotional effectiveness of official media—television, radio and newspapers—are unmatched anywhere else in the world. The official media, for instance, have millions and sometimes over a billion loyal listeners, viewers or readers. Hence, despite the high fees, substantial investment in promotion and public relations, including advertisements, is truly a wise use of resources. However, if you invest only a small sum in promotion in the Chinese market, it will have little or no effect. According to the Chinese proverb it will be like 'throwing a handful of salt into the sea to make it more salty'. Added to this is the promotional cost of breaking into regional sales networks, which is also very costly.

Besides this, there are also intangible expenses—fees for the establishment and maintenance of business relationships. Non-productive expenses such as gift-giving or treating guests are costly in China. In a formal accounting system, this type of expense may not be counted as a legitimate business deduction against Western-based taxation. However, owing to the characteristics of Chinese business culture, any foreign company operating in China must be prepared to allocate capital resources to public relations, otherwise complete failure will be ensured. The manager of a public relations department of a Chinese company, or even the general manager, is often authorised to use a certain amount of money for 'building business relationships'.

The Chinese Government usually offers more favourable concessions to large companies that have strong financial backing, although it welcomes all foreign investment. Large companies with international reputations can easily catch the attention of the Chinese Government at all levels, leading to the dual advantages of financial protection and political support.

Predisposition: Preparation in Business Policy and Social Relationships

Previous chapters have demonstrated that China's social and economic systems are different from those of other countries, and that China's business culture is unique. These conditions require you to be fully briefed about all relevant government policies. It also requires you to establish sound commercial and interpersonal relationships at the beginning of any business venture in China.

Understanding specific government industry policies

Collecting, interpreting and understanding information about Chinese governmental industry policy is essential preparation for foreign investors in the Chinese market. Since the government is still the predominant controller of the Chinese economy, there are either limiting and or favourable policies stipulated by the government that could profoundly influence operational performance. Failure to fully appreciate a particular policy can lead to commercial disaster, whereas being fully conversant with current policy trends can minimise risk by making use of supportive industry initiatives.

Knowing your business partners

If you are planning to commit your capital to a joint venture in China, you need to first invest time and energy in acquiring information about your potential partners. You must determine their personal and professional strengths and weakness, and in addition understand thoroughly the project's ownership, financial power and nature. You need to analyse relevant data to identify suitable partners for your business. Each of the four types of ownership described in Chapter 5 is linked to specific advantages and disadvantages of various aspects of obtaining governmental support, including financial backup, market orientation and assistance programmes to increase industrial performance and the transfer and possession of technology.

You need to carefully determine whether your partner has sufficient financial strength to meet long-term financial or organisational commitments. A Chinese enterprise or company may possess excellent technical staff or skilled workers, but may not have the financial capacity to complete the joint venture project on time or see it through to completion. However, in order to attract a foreign company's investment, a few Chinese managers may fail to mention their own financial weaknesses, possibly out of a sense of embarrassment, or it may be a deliberate ploy to convince you of their worthiness by drawing attention to other non-financial advantages. They will usually inform you of their difficult financial situation after both sides have invested substantial amounts of capital into the project, and as a result, force you to continually invest more and more capital into the same project by making use of your desperate desire not to lose previous gains. Chinese businesspeople call this a 'fishing project', which means they use some of their advantages as 'bait' to catch a large investor. Although there are only a few Chinese enterprises that practise this tactic, you must avoid being trapped into such a one-sided relationship by carrying out investigations before investing.

Building up a business relationship

Every enterprise in China must identify and establish a relationship with relevant Chinese officials, suppliers and other businesspeople. This can be likened to an insurance policy. Like all insurance, the premium must be paid before risk is taken and an accident occurs. Business relationships in China, on the other hand, take a long time to build up and a great deal of care to maintain. The important point is that these relationships are reciprocal—they should operate for mutual benefit. Chinese in both the business world and in the bureaucratic system do not appreciate being approached for assistance only when it is convenient or useful to their foreign counterpart. In such a case they would feel that they are being treated as a tool, and may be reluctant to offer further assistance.

Document preparation

Due to the barriers of language and culture, a company's documents must be prepared in advance in both the English and Chinese languages. This preparation results in a streamlining of the negotiating process, which in turn reduces the potential for misunderstandings to develop. In China a foreigner may easily find a Chinese national who has reasonable English language speaking skills. However, it is difficult to find a native Chinese speaker who is a qualified oral interpreter, fluent in writing as well as speaking English. It is even more difficult to find a qualified interpreter who is able to understand the subtleties of both Chinese and Western business cultures.

Personnel: Recruiting the Right People

The importance of recruiting the right people has been raised in a number of earlier chapters. Finding skilled, experienced and trustworthy local people who are capable of exploring business and/or social relationships for the purpose of commerce is the key to success in China. As a new entrant to the market, you should consider this point carefully, especially if you intend to operate as a wholly-owned foreign enterprise. You have the disadvantage of not having a Chinese partner who can provide the necessary local cultural knowledge or practical business experience to minimise risk. A successful foreign company in China must be one that can master the traits of Chinese business culture by either choosing the right partner or by employing the right people.

Throughout the previous chapters we have argued that Chinese business culture is not only about professional knowledge, technology, or the skills of business, but also includes many extra-commercial, sociological or cultural affairs as well. A foreigner or expatriate may master Chinese etiquette, language, political culture or economic policy by living in China for many years. However, you may still have difficulties in fully comprehending the psychology of the Chinese people, and so will continue to struggle with complex, culturally based business issues. It can never be said that a foreigner could understand the subtle cultural nuances and psychological traits of the Chinese people better than a native resident.

At present, some offices or branches of large foreign companies in China have already taken advantage of local knowledge by appointing Chinese nationals as senior managers, and relied on them to effectively promote and develop company business in the Chinese market. A foreign executive manager has summarised this matter thus: 'A businessperson needs people who know people, who can make decisions. In a country as diverse as China, without *guanxi* ['connections'], without language skills or local knowledge, a foreigner will never find the keys to the Celestial Kingdom's marketplace.'

The most suitable person to explore business in China could be defined as one who has experience in dealing with both the local bureaucracy and media, and also has knowledge of the relevant professional field. On most occasions, experience in dealing with social matters is more important than professional knowledge. In Chinese business culture an employee in a key or senior position must not only know the traits of Chinese business culture, but must also be able to deal confidently with any issue by drawing on their extensive practical experience. The following story illustrates this.

A foreign company failed to develop business in China as a result of appointing an unsuitable person. The company placed a recruitment advertisement in their home country seeking a native Chinese to develop their business in the Chinese market. The advertisement outlined a number of employment principles, including holding a higher degree in a related special field, professional knowledge in a technical area and bilingual language competency. In return the company offered an attractive salary package.

A Chinese person who had worked overseas was appointed according to the terms and conditions set out in the advertisement. He was then sent back to China to explore the market on behalf of this foreign-owned technology company. This man was indeed both knowledgeable and experienced in his field of expertise, but had no idea whatsoever about the current state of Chinese commerce and was not familiar with the important commercial centres of Beijing, Shanghai and Guangzhou, since he had been studying and working in laboratories overseas. He did not have the practical experience to deal with Chinese officials, nor the necessary connections to establish professional relationships on behalf of his foreign company. As a result, after one year there was still no substantive progress. The hapless employee could find no way of effectively contacting the relevant governmental or commercial officials. The lesson to be learned is that foreign companies operating in China must be flexible enough to recruit employees who are fully versed in the main aspects of Chinese business culture, formal and informal, technical and intuitive.

From the perspective of labour training programmes for workers, this advice is also relevant and important. You must be flexible about training new employees. The average Chinese worker is very disciplined and hard-working, and possesses reasonable skills. However, at present these same workers may have an underdeveloped sense of efficiency and participation, compared to workers in some developed countries. Cultural values such as the 'Iron Rice Bowl' of state-owned organisations still exert a powerful influence on Chinese workers. Associated problems, such as a poor appreciation of quality control, can be overcome by initiating a comprehensive training programme to improve the performance and outlook of Chinese workers at the very beginning of a particular joint venture or foreign-owned enterprise project. You can thus achieve twice the outcome for half the effort. The alternative is to respond to problems ineffectually as they arise, rather that enact real cultural and workplace reform.

Protection: Legal Protection

The legal system in China is still far from easy to work with, although in recent years many new Laws and Acts have been issued. Some Chinese businesspeople have no sense of the importance of the rule of law. Besides the usual problems that occur from time to time between labour and management anywhere in the world, troubles such as violating contracts, bribery, corruption, violations against trademark rights and embezzlement happen in China. To protect the rights and interests of business in China, every foreign and Chinese businessperson needs to know how to handle a range of negative commercial activities.

You should know everything possible about a Chinese company or agency you are going to deal with, including the personal details about the managers and executives involved in the project. One of the crucial questions is, who is administratively in charge of business, that is, which level of government supervises negotiations, and then which government department and which particular government officer will be responsible for the project after negotiations are complete.

Make sure the type and full extent of protection is available under Chinese law, and that the policy afforded to a particular project or trade item is applied fairly.

Sign contracts with a partner or new employees before you begin formal business cooperation; include items in the written contract that cover rights and responsibilities, in both Chinese and English. A process for settling disputes must also be worked out in advance and then written into the contract.

In China, there are four types of organisation that offer foreign companies legal assistance: the Foreign Economic and Trade Arbitration Commission, the Commission for Discipline Inspection of the Communist Party (at both the central and local levels) and the Foreign Traders' Association. In addition, there are qualified and competent solicitors or attorneys in every regional area.

Perspective: Cultural Sensitivity

China is an immature market, but it is growing up at a phenomenal rate. The administrative and cultural change that took over 200 years to fashion the practice of a distinctive mode of Western and now international business culture has all but been achieved in China in one generation. It is beyond dispute that what China now requires is a strong and enforceable rule of law, bureaucratic transparency and administrative predictability. Equally, it is now beyond question that if China continues on the path of economic reform (in an atmosphere of political and social stability) then the Great Dragon will reach its potential as the powerhouse of the world's economy in the 21st century.

The astute businessperson can use the six P's to evaluate China's incalculable potential. You can then culturally, financially and technically prepare yourself for successful commerce and trade in the world's largest market.

Chinese Business Almanac

What now makes China unique in the world of investment is that its businesspeople have so far weathered the 1997–98 Asian financial crisis. One of the reasons why it has not suffered as badly as other Asian countries is that its economic fundamentals and reform policy are considered to be basically on the right track by the International Monetary Fund (IMF) and the World Bank. Evidence of this is that the reform policies of the late Deng Xiao Ping have produced an annual average growth rate in GDP of 9% over 18 years since 1979. Part of the reason for this is that China's exports have grown from US$18.27 billion in 1980 to US$ 151.1 billion in 1996, an increase of 8.27 times, with total imports and exports presently running at US$325 billion (1997)—the world's ninth most successful trading nation.

In 1996, with its growth rate of GDP at 9.7%, China's domestic investment in fixed assets was measured at US$284.68 billion. This increase of 18.2% from 1995 is due partly to China's outstanding national savings record, which in 1997 reached US$464.41 billion.

Attracting foreign capital has been an important aspect of China's reform policy. Consequently, China is now the world's fastest-growing economy, and one of the world's most attractive markets for capital investment. In the period between 1980 and 1997, China attracted a total of US$212.12 billion in capital investment from a staggering 300 000 foreign joint venture companies. Moreover, contracted investment is currently running at US$510 billion. According to a report from the Trade and Development Section of the United Nations, China is now ranked second place in the world, behind the United States, in terms of capital inflow. As a result, in 1997 the Chinese Government achieved an 8.8% growth rate of GDP and US$305.1 billion in domestic investment of fixed assets. Since then China's foreign exchange reserve has reached US$140 billion at the end of 1997, ranking second in the world after Japan.

The Natural and Human Geography of China

Provinces, Cities with Provincial Status, and Autonomous Regions

Provinces

Province	Area (sq. km)	Population (millions)	Capital
Anhui	140 000	50	Hefei
Fujian	121 700	26	Fuzhou
Gansu	450 000	20	Lanzhou
Guangdong	212 000	61	Guangzhou
Guizhou	174 000	28	Guiyang
Hainan	34 000	6	Haikou
Hebei	187 700	54	Shijiazhuang
Heilongjiang	469 000	33.1	Harbin
Hubei	187 000	48	Wuhan
Hunan	167 000	75	Zhenzhou
Hunan[1]	210 000	55.1	Changsha
Jiangsu	102 600	60.2	Nanjing
Jiangxi	166 600	32	Nanchang
Jilin	180 000	23	Changchun
Liaoning	145 740	36.3	Shenyang
Quinghai	720 000	4	Xining
Shanxi	195 800	29.1	Xian

Business Culture in China

Province	Area (sq. km)	Population (millions)	Capital
Shanxi[1]	156 000	25.5	Taiyuan
Shandong	153 300	74	Jinan
Sichuan	570 000	69.8	Chengdu
Taiwan	35 788	21	Taibei
Zhejiang	101 800	38.9	Hangzhou

[1] The name of this province has the same pronunciation as the one above, but is spoken using a different tone and is written with a different Chinese character.

Cities with Provincial Status

City	Area (sq. km)	Population (millions)
Beijing	16 800	9.4
Chiqing	82 000	30.2
Shanghai	6 186	12
Tianjin	11 000	7

Autonomous Regions

Region	Area (sq. km)	Population (millions)	Capital
Guangxi Zhuang	230 000	40.2	Nanning
Inner Mongolia	1 100 000	20.3	Hohehot
Ningxia Huiziu	660 000	4.2	Yinchuan
Tibet	1 200 000	2	Lhasa
Xinjiang	1 600 000	13.8	Urumqi

Special Administrative Zone

Zone	Area (sq km.)	Polulation (millions)
Hong Kong	1 000	6

Chinese Language

Chinese is a family of languages as diverse as the Romance languages of Europe. China's main dialects are not mutually comprehensible in tone. There are ten major dialects in China, including Mandarin, Cantonese, Shanghaiese, Fukienese, Hokkien, Hakka and Chin Chow. Among them, Mandarin (or *Putonghua* in Mandarin) is the official language. This is the language of education, commerce and national broadcasting. It is currently estimated that some 75% of China's younger population understands and speaks Mandarin. Despite the fact that the various dialects are mostly made up of different words with different pronunciations, practically all variations of the one basic Chinese language use exactly the same ideographic writing system, in which most of the individual characters have the same meaning. Chinese people, regardless of their dialect, can read each others' writing.

There are also significant differences between spoken and written Chinese and between informal and 'official' language. Informal spoken Chinese is very casual, with special nuances that are difficult or impossible for non-Chinese to fully grasp. In formal or official situations, spoken Chinese becomes very stylised and refined. It requires great skill and experience to use properly.

Because of these language differences, be wary of engaging in idle chatter, particularly during business discussions. It is important to use simple, straightforward terms, in English or in Mandarin, that lend themselves to direct translation and reduce the possibility of misunderstandings.

Climate

Because of its vast territory and wide range of altitudes, China's climate varies considerably in different regions. Most of China's land lies in the northern temperate zone, and enjoys four distinct seasons. Generally speaking, January is the coldest month and July is the warmest. The climate of Northern China, in the temperate zone, is arid; while Southern China, in the subtropical zone, is humid.

Some Economic Information

Chinese and Foreign Trade Promotion Organisations

American Chamber of Commerce
   Rm 444, Great Wall Sheraton Hotel, Beijing
   Tel: 86-10-65005566-271

Beijing Overseas Service Center
   36 Dong Si, Xi Da Jie, Beijing
   Tel: 86-10-65124589

Beijing Service Company for Investment and Trade from Taiwan Compatriots
5 Building, Xi Huang Cheng Gen Nan Jie Yi Qu, Beijing
Tel: 86-10-66032811

British Chamber of Commerce in China
31 Technical Club, 15 Guanghuali, Jianguomenwai, Beijing
Tel: 86-10-65936611/12/13; 86-10-65017788 ext. 255/6/7/8.

Canada–China Business Council
18-2 CITIC Building, 19 Jian Guo Men Wai Da Jie, Beijing
Tel: 86-10-65126120; 86-10-65002255 - 1820, 1821
Fax: 86-10-65126125.

China Council for the Promotion of International Trade, Beijing Branch
4/F, Second Part, Middle Building, Hua Long Jie, Nan He Yan, Beijing
Tel: 86-10-65125175

China–Italy Chamber of Commerce
Rm. No. 301 Guanghuayuan Building, No. 38 Donghuan Beilu, Beijing
Tel: 86-10-65069481

French Chamber of Commerce & Industry
12/F Guang Ming Hotel, Liang Ma Qiao Lu, Beijing
Tel: 86-10-65016896

Fu Xing Men Wai Da Jie, Beijing
Tel: 86-10-68513344

Hong Kong Trade & Development Council
Rm. 9, 8 Bright China Changan Building, 7 Jiannei Da Jie, Beijing
Tel: 86-10-65101700

Italian Institute for Foreign Trade
3041, Jingguang Center, Beijing
Tel: 86-10-65003369
Fax: 86-10-65012884

Japan–China Association on Economy & Trade & Japan–China Long-Term Trade Committee, Beijing Office
401 Chang Fu Gong Office Building, Jian Guo Men Wai, Beijing
Tel: 65129880. 65129881
Fax: 86-10-65129884

Japanese Chamber
104 Chang Fu Gong Office Building, Jian Guo Men Wai, Beijing
Tel: 86-10-65130129
Fax: 86-10-65139859

South African Center for Chinese Studies
C801, Lufthunsa Center, Beijing
Tel: 86-10-64651941

United States–China Business Council
22-C CITIC Building, 19 Jian Guo Men Wai Da Jie, Beijing

Tel: 86-10-65002255-2263, 2266
Fax: 86-10-65125854

China's Top Ten Import and Export Corporations (1997)

China National Chemicals Import & Export Corporation
Tel: 86-10-68568888 Fax: 86-10-68568890

China National Cereals, Oils & Foodstuffs Import & Export Corporation
Tel: 86-10-65268888
Fax: 86-10-65276044

China National Technical Import & Export Corporation
Tel: 86-10-68404000
Fax: 86-10-68414877

China Petrochemical International Company
Tel: 86-10-64911594
Fax: 86-10-64216972

China National Metals & Minerals Import & Export Corporation
Tel: 86-10-64916666
Fax:86-10-64917031

China National Textiles Import & Export Corporation
Tel: 86-10-65124707
Fax: 86-10-65124711

China National Electronics Import & Export Corporation
Tel: 86-10-68219550
Fax: 86-10-68212352

China National Machinery Import & Export Corporation
Tel: 86-10-68494812
Fax: 86-10-68317962

China Iron & Steel Industry & Trade Group Corporation
Tel: 86-10-65220752
Fax: 86-10-65123792

China North Industries Corporation
Tel: 86-10-63529988
Fax: 86-10-63540398

Top Ten Provinces and Cities in Terms of Total Import and Export Trade

Based on organisational operating location.

'95	Province or City	US$ billion	'96	Province or City	US$ billion
1	GuangDong	103.9	1	GuangDong	121.7
2	Beijing	37	2	ShangHai	52.9

'95	Province or City	US$ billion	'96	Province or City	US$ billion
3	ShangHai	24.3	3	TianJing	21.5
4	JiangSu	16.3	4	ShanDong	18.7
5	FuJian	14.4	5	LiaoNing	17.1
6	ShanDong	13.9	6	FuJian	14.1
7	LiaoNingıo	13.2	7	JiangSu	12.4
8	ZheJiang	11.5	8	ZheJiang	7.9
9	TianJing	8	9	Beijing	5.7
10	HeBei	3.9	10	HeBei	2.5

Categories of Export Sales

Reported by The China Customs Bureau.

Rank	Category	Export sales in 1995 US$(billion)	Export sales in 1996 US$(billion)
1	Textile and finished garments	35.878	34.969
2	Machinery; electronic equipment and spare parts; video recorders, equipment and spare parts	27.667	31.065
3	Precious metals and end products	12.081	10.407
4	Chemical products	8.421	8.427
5	Shoes, hats, umbrellas, feathers and feather products	8.159	8.545

Top Ten Principal Trading Partners in 1997

1	Japan	6	Taiwan
2	Hong Kong	7	Singapore
3	America	8	Russia
4	European Union	9	Australia
5	Korea	10	Indonesia

Information Services

China Foreign Economic & Trade Consultant Company
12 B Guanghua Lu, Jian Guo Men Wai Da Jie, Beijing
Tel: 86-10-65052255

SinoFile Information Services
Tonglinge Street, Xicheng District, Beijing
Tel: 86-10-66059198 Fax: 86-10-66059194

State Information Centre
58 San Li He Lu, Beijing
Tel: 86-10-68528701

Banks and Financial Institutions

The Agricultural Bank of China, Beijing Branch
15 Shui Dan Zi Hu Tong,Tian Tan Dong Me
Tel: 86-10-67014233

ANZ Banking Group Ltd
17th Floor, Tower 2, Beijing Bright China Chang An Building
No.7 Jian Guo Men Nei Avenue, Dong Cheng An Building
Tel: 86-10-6510 2929
Fax: 86-10-6510 2920

Banco Santander
Unit 2301, Landmark Building
Tel: 86-10-65068021

Bank of America
Rm. 2609, China World Tower, Beijing
Tel: 86-10-65053508

Bank of Tokyo-Mitsubishi
2/F Fortune Building, Beijing
Tel: 86-10-65931640

Banque Nationale de Paris
China World Tower, Beijing
Tel: 86-10-65053685

Barclays Bank
SCITE Tower, Beijing
Tel: 86-10-65122288 ext.1211

Citibank
CITIC Building, Beijing
Tel: 86-10-65002255 ext. 1810

CITIC Industrial Bank
6 Xin Yuan Nan Lu
86-1-65122233

Deutsche Bank
China World Tower
Tel: 86-10-65052306

Hong Kong and Shanghai Bank
  Jianguo Hotel, Beijing
  Tel: 86-10-65001121

The Industrial & Commercial Bank of China, Beijing Branch
  10 Bai Yan Lu, Beijing
  Tel: 86-10-63409922

The People's Bank of China, Beijing Branch
  9 Xi He Yan, Qian Men
  Tel: 86-10-63035254. 86-10-65199437

The People's Construction Bank of China, Beijing Branch
  A1 Ma Lian Duo Bei Lu, Guang An Men Wai
  Tel: 86-10-63265301

State Administration of Exchange Control, Beijing Branch, Regulatory
  Center
  79 Yue Tan Nan Jie, Beijing
  Tel: 86-10-68572108Standard Chartered Bank
  Hong Kong Macao Center
  Tel: 86-10-65011578

Swiss Bank Corporation
  Rm. 3624, China World Tower, Beijing
  Tel: 86-10-65052213

Embassies

Embassy of Australia
  21 Dong Zhi Men Wai Da Jie, San Li Tun, Beijing
  Tel: 86-10-65322331
  Austrade Commercial Office Tel: 86-10-65326726-6731

Embassy of Canada
  19 Dong Zhi Men Wai Da Jie, Beijing
  Tel: 86-10-65323536

Royal Danish Embassy
  1 Dong Wu Kie, San Li Tun, Beijing
  Tel: 86-10-65322431

Embassy of the Republic of Finland
  1-10-1 Ta Yuan Office Building, Beijing
  Tel: 86-10-65321817
  Commercial Office: 7/F Dong Hu Office Building, Beijing Tel: 86-10-
  64678084.

Embassy of the Republic of France
  3 Dong San Jie, San Li Tun
  Tel: 86-10-65321331
  Commercial Office: 37/F Jing Guang Center, Beijing Tel: 86-10-
  65014866.

Embassy of the Federal Republic of Germany
5 Dong Zhi Men Wai Da Jie, Beijing
Tel: 86-10-: 65325557
Commercial Office: 3 San Li Tun, Dong Si Jie, Beijing Tel: 86-10-65325556

Embassy of the Republic of Hungary
10 Dong Zhi Men Wai Da Jie, Beijing
Tel: 86-10-65321431
Commercial Office: 5-2-151 Ta Yuan Apartment, Beijing Tel: 86-10-65323182

Embassy of the Republic of India
1 Ri Tan Dong Lu, Beijing
Tel: 86-10-65321856

Embassy of the Republic of Indonesia
Office Building B, San Li Tun, Beijing
Tel 86-10-65325488

Embassy of the Republic of Italy
2 Dong Er Jie, Sun Li Tun
Tel: 86-10-65322131

Embassy of Japan
7 Ri Tan Lu, Jian Guo Men Wai, Beijing
Tel: 86-10-65322361

Embassy of the Republic of Korea
4/F China World Tower, 1 Jian Guo Men Wai Da Jie, Beijing
Tel: 86-10-65052608

Embassy of Mongolia
2 Xiu Shui Bei Jie, Fian Guo Men Wai, Beijing
Tel: 86-10-65321203

Royal Netherlands Embassy
1-15-2 Ta Yuan Office Building, Beijing
Tel: 86-10-65321131

Embassy of New Zealand
1 Dong Er Jie, Ri Tan Lu, Beijing
Tel: 86-10-65322261

Embassy of Republic of the Philippines
23 Xiu Shui Bei Jie, Jian Guo Men Wai, Beijing
Tel: 86-10-65322794

Embassy of Republic of Poland
1 Ri Tan Lu, Jian Gou Men Wai, Beijing
Tel: 86-10-65321235

Embassy of the Republic of Portugal
2-72 San Li Tun Office Building, Beijing
Tel: 86-10-65323497

Embassy of Romania
Ri Tan Lu, Dong Er Jie, Beijing
Tel: 86-10-65323442

Embassy of the Russian Federation
4 Dong Zhi Men Bei Zhong Jie, Beijing
Tel: 86-10-65322051

Embassy of the Republic of Singapore
1 Xiu Shui Bei Jie, Jian Guo Men Wai, Beijing
Tel: 86-10-65323926

Embassy of Spain
9 San Li Tun Lu, Beijing
Tel: 86-10-65323629
Commercial Section: 2-2-2 Ta Yuan Office Building, Beijing Tel: 86-10-65322072

Embassy of Sweden
3 Dong Zhi Men Wai Da Jie, Beijing
Tel: 86-10-65323331

Embassy of Switzerland
3 Dong Wu Jie, San Li Tun, Beijing
Tel: 86-10-65322736

Royal Thai Embassy
40 Guang Hua Lu, Beijing
Tel: 86-10-65321903

Embassy of the United Kingdom of Great Britain and Northern Ireland
11 Guang Hua Lu, Beijing
Tel: 86-10-65321961

Embassy of the United States of America
3 Xiu Shui Bei Jie, Jian Guo Men Wai, Beijing
Tel: 86-10-65323831

Hotel Accommodation

Top Ten Hotels in Beijing
Telephone area code: 86-10

Hotel name	Telephone no.	Fax no.
Bei Jing Hotel	65137766	65137842
China World Hotel	65052266	65053167
Grand Hotel Beijing	65137788	65130048
Great Wall Sheraton Hotel	65005566	65005222
Jing Guang New World Hotel	65018888	65013333
Kun Lun Hotel	65003388	65003228

Hotel name	Telephone no.	Fax no.
New Otani Chang Fu Gong Hotel	65125555	65125346
Palace Hotel	65128899	65129050
Shangrila Hotel Beijing	68412211	68418002
Wang Fu Jing Grand Hotel	65221188	65223749

Top Ten Hotels in Shanghai
Telephone area code: 86-12

Hotel name	Telephone no.	Fax no.
Equatorial Hotel	62481688	62484393
Galaxy Hotel	62755888	62750039
Garden Hotel	64151111	64158866
Hua Ting Hotel	64391000	64390130
Jin Jiang Tower	64151188	64150048
Mandarin Hotel	62791888	62791822
Park Hotel	63275225	63276958
Peace Hotel	63216888	63290300
Portman & Higrala Hotel	62798888	62798800
The Yangtze Hotel	62750000	62750750

Top Ten Hotels in GuangZhou
Telephone area code: 86-20

Hotel name	Telephone no.	Fax no.
Central Hotel	86678331	86663191
China Hotel	86666888	86677014
Dong Fang Hotel	86669900	86662775
The Garden Hotel	83338989	83350467
Guang Dong Guest House	83332950	83332911
Hotel Landmark Canton	83355988	83336197
HuaTai Hotel	87789888	87788118
Novotel GuangzhouJiangnan	84418888	84429645
White Swan Hotel	81886968	81861188
Yuexiu Tian'an Mansion	86665666	86671741

Business Culture in China

Telephone Information Services

Information about telephone numbers	114
Time check	117
Information about the weather	121
Information about postcodes	63037031

Telephone Numbers of Airlines in Beijing

Capital Airport Information	64563604
Air France	65051818
Alitalia	65014861
Austrian Airlines	65917861
British Airways	65124080
Canadian Airlines	64637901
China Airlines (International)	66016667
Pakistan International	65050088
Dragonair	65054343
Finer	65127180
Garuda Indonesia	64561686
Iran Air	65124940
Japan Airlines	65130888
Korean Air	65051047
Lufthansa	64654488
Malaysia Airlines	65052682
Northeast Airlines	65050505
Polish Airlines	65007215
Qantas	64674794
Romanian Air Transport	65002233
SAS	65120575
Singapore Airlines	65052233
Swissair	65123555
Thai International	64608899
United Airlines	64631111
Yugoslav Airlines	65952166

Currency Exchange Rates
24 September 1997

The Chinese currency is the *reminbi yuan*, often written as *RMB yuan*.

Country or Place	One unit of currency	One *RMB* *yuan* is worth
Australia	1 dollar	0.17
Britain	1 pound	0.07
Canada	1 dollar	0.17
Europe	1 ecu	0.11
France	1 franc	0.72
India	1 rupee	4.38
Germany	1 mark	0.22
Hong Kong	1 dollar	0.93
Indonesia	100 rupiah	362
Japan	100 yen	14
Malaysia	1 ringgit	0.37
Mexico	1 new peso	0.93
New Zealand	1 dollar	0.19
Russia	100 ruble	706
Singapore	1 dollar	0.18
South Korea	100 won	362
Switzerland	1 franc	0.18
Taiwan	1 N.T. dollar	3.46
United States	1 dollar	0.12

Source: *Asiaweek* October 3, 1997.

Index

F

'face protection'
banquets, 61
gift-giving, 109
importance, 22, 23–24
negotiations, 53–55, 57
saying 'No', 38–39
'family' hierarchy
enterprise organisation, 72–73
societal hierarchy, 20–21
feasibility studies, 84
feng shui, 39–40
financial control, 97–98
financial institutions, 181–182
'flaunting' consumption,
121–123
foreign businesses
advertising rates, 148–149
intangible costs, 167
loans, 97–98
management recruitment, 88
types, 80–81
foreign investment
basic industries, 133–134
contracted amount, 175
government control, 98–100
growth, 15
foreign trade, 29–30
form of address, 103
formal introductions, 48
fortune, good, 39–41
friendships *see* relationships

G

GDP (gross domestic product)
China, 14, 15, 174
Shanghai, 13
geography
autonomous regions, 176
cities with provincial status,
176
provinces, 175–176

Special Administrative Zone,
176
gift-giving
corrupt officials, 111–113
'face-protection', 108–109
government officials, 109–110
luxury goods, 120–121
opening etiquette, 110
packaging, 121, 141–143
social role, 108–109
'Golden Currency Projects, The',
129
'Golden Customs Projects, The',
129
'Golden Tax Projects, The', 129
'good guy and bad guy' tactic,
67–68
government officials
effective communication,
101–108
financial control, 97–98
foreign investment control,
98–100
form of address, 103
friendships, 103, 106–107
gifts, 109–110
joint venture cooperation, 96
large enterprise management,
98
need for good relationship,
94–95
price control, 96–97
respect for, 102–103
role, 100
treating as a network,
105–108
'grey income', 125–126
gross domestic product (GDP)
China, 14, 15, 174
Shanghai, 13
group purchases, non-
productive, 127–128
guanxi ('connections'), 75, 103,
170–171
Gunboat diplomacy, 11–12

non-competitive, 74
old school, 88, 90–91
parallel systems, 71–72
performance based, 80
workplace harmony, 75–76
managers
middle, 77, 91–92
senior, 90–91, 170
successful qualities, 89
marketing research
choosing an organisation,
137–138
consultancy proposals, 138
need for, 136–137
obtaining commercial data,
136–137
MBA degrees, 87–88
media categories, 143–146
meetings, formal, 77
middle managers
dealing with, 91–92
decision-making, 77
'Mind Liberalisation', 13–14
Ming Dynasty, 9
mobile phones, 129
moral norms, 22

N

national pride, 3–4
negotiations
characteristics, 46–58
discussion rounds, 50
'face protection', 53–55
final stage, 55–58
informal setting, 61
initial stage, 46–50
middle stage, 50–55
need for style, 45
objectives, 52
post-contract, 56
premature end, 53–54
prolonged, 51
role of banquets *see* banquets

roles within teams, 46–49
starting with interpersonal relationships, 49–50
tactics, 65–69
terminating, 57–58
networks
business relationships, 36–37
government officials, 105–108
newspapers
advertising rates, 148–149
central government owner-
ship, 144, 145
powerful position, 154–155
'No', saying, 38–39
non-productive group purchases,
127–128
numbers, lucky, 40–41

O

obedience, 75
office rental, 166
officialdom *see* bureaucracy
one-child policy
consumer psychology, 124
influence on purchases,
118–120
Open Door policy, 8, 13–15,
31–32, 34, 86, 161
opium trade, 10–11

P

packaging, 141–143
partners
finding, 81–83
selecting, 168–169
patience, 50, 51, 68, 162–165
personal appearance, 39, 41
personal computer market,
130–131
personnel recruitment, 86–89,
169–172

Business Culture in China

perspective, cultural, 173
'physiognomy', 39, 41
policies, understanding,
    167–168
political issues, discussion of,
    101–102
population
  autonomous regions, 176
  cities with provincial status,
    176
  one-child policy, 118–119
  provinces, 175–176
  Special Administrative Zone,
    176
  urban, 17
  world's largest market, 16
power
  financial, 166–167
  newspapers, 154–155
  public shows of, 53–55
  purchasing, 114–115, 125
predisposition, policies and rela-
    tionships, 167–169
preparation
  policies and relationships,
    167–169
  psychological, 162–165
price control, 96–97
privately owned enterprises, 28,
    82–83
product placement, 155
profits, desire for, 33–34
programme sponsorship, 155
promotion
  advertising, 143–149
  branding, 138–140
  packaging, 141–143
  public relations role, 149–153
proposals, business, 84
protection, legal, 172–173
public relations
  consultative, 151
  growing acceptance, 149–150
  'public good' oriented,
    152–153

publicity-oriented, 150–151
  skills required, 153
  socially oriented, 151
publicity, 154–155
purchasing power, 114–115,
    125

Q

Qing Dynasty, 10–12, 29
quality control, 91

R

radio advertising, 144
recruitment, staff, 86–89,
    169–172
'red face and white face' tactic,
    67–68
relationships
  based on amicability, 34–35
  based on obedience, 75
  beginning negotiations, 49–50
  building, 169
  business value, 35–37
  five basic categories, 21
  government officials, 103,
    106–107, 109–110
  informal, 75–76
  role of banquets, 60
retail outlets, 160

S

salaries
  levels, 126
  payment system, 73
saving face *see* 'face protection'
savings
  national, 16, 174
  pre-purchase, 115–116
seal, official, 37–38

194